THIS BOOK BELONGS TO:

....

CHRISTMAS 2017

2017

CHRISTMAS

—— WITH ——

Southern Living

2017
CHRISTMAS
WITH
Southern Living

INSPIRED IDEAS FOR
HOLIDAY COOKING AND DECORATING

Oxmoor House

MERRY CHRISTMAS!

We welcome you to flip through the pages of the 2017 edition of *Christmas with Southern Living* to find inspiration for a season of gatherings. You'll find page after page of decorating ideas for decking the halls, mantel, and banister too, as well as every nook and cranny in between. We take the pressure off holiday meal planning with 100 all-new, kitchen-tested recipes for relaxing weeknight meals with family or festive holiday feasts for a crowd. Our kitchen staff shares pretty fantastic ideas for utilizing leftovers or, as we prefer to call them, "Bestovers" based on recipes from the menus you'll find inside. With ideas for cooking and decorating, giving, serving, and wrapping, we've got Christmas covered from start to finish.

Thanks for letting us into your home this holiday season.

Katherine Cobbs

Katherine Cobbs
Senior Editor

CONTENTS

Entertain 8

Savor 98

Share 154

ENTERTAIN

CHRISTMAS
on the farm

*As autumn gives way to winter, we usher in the
holiday season. It's time for family and friends
to come together to celebrate around a farmstead
menu that bridges the seasons.*

THE MENU
serves 8 to 10

MONTGOMERY MULE

BUTTERNUT SQUASH-PEAR-
PROSCIUTTO PARCELS

ROASTED CELERY-
FENNEL SOUP

KALE-AND-ESCAROLE
SALAD WITH PARSNIPS
AND DRIED CRANBERRIES

BRINED AND BLASTED
TURKEY WITH
GINGER-ROSEMARY
CRANBERRY SAUCE

CREAMED SWISS CHARD
WITH ZESTY WALNUT
TOPPING

HASSELBACK POTATO
CASSEROLE WITH COMTÉ
AND BACON

WHOLE ROASTED CARROTS
WITH HONEY AND HERBS

DEEP-DISH APPLE-
SWEET POTATO PIE WITH
MAPLE ICE CREAM

MAKE A DISH

A collection of heirloom pieces combined with greenery adds festive flair to a rustic hutch. More platters and plates orbit a bovine beauty accented with a magnolia wreath.

TINSEL AND TRANSFERWARE

Heirloom collections enlisted into service as the backdrop for holiday decorating make great conversation pieces. A tiered stand becomes a catchall for packages ready for delivery, while an antique scale, breadbox, and water pitcher form an interesting tableau in the kitchen. A collection of ironstone and green-and-white transferware inspires the palette, while a mix of evergreen boughs and tarnished silver candlesticks with flickering candles add interest. Gray brunia berries, white tulips, and roses give easy looseness to arrangements for a perfect dose of casual elegance.

Montgomery Mule, Butternut Squash-
Pear-Prosciutto Parcels

Kale-and-Escarole Salad with Parsnips and
Dried Cranberries, Roasted Celery-Fennel Soup

Clockwise from below: Whole Roasted Carrots with Honey
and Herbs, Creamed Swiss Chard with Zesty Walnut Topping,
Brined and Blasted Turkey, Ginger-Rosemary Cranberry Sauce,
Hasselback Potato Casserole with Comté and Bacon

Deep-Dish Apple-Sweet Potato
Pie with Maple Ice Cream

Montgomery Mule

Chartreuse, a French liqueur, gives this cocktail an herbaceous edge while Alabama's spicy Buffalo Rock ginger ale adds a decidedly Southern twist—one that gives this spin on the Moscow Mule its name. Serve in a glass or a more traditional copper mug.

SERVES 1

HANDS-ON 5 MINUTES

TOTAL 5 MINUTES

⅓ cup (about 3 ounces) vodka

⅓ cup spicy ginger ale (such as Buffalo Rock)

1 tablespoon fresh lemon juice (from ½ lemon)

1 teaspoon yellow Chartreuse

1 teaspoon simple syrup

Lemon peel strip (optional)

Combine vodka, ginger ale, lemon juice, Chartreuse, and simple syrup in a cocktail glass or copper mug filled with ice. Garnish with lemon peel strip, if desired.

Butternut Squash-Pear-Prosciutto Parcels

This clever idea for a pickup appetizer is a celebration of seasonal ingredients. It helps to have a very sharp chef's knife for cutting through the tough skin of winter squash. A serrated grapefruit spoon makes scraping out seeds a cinch.

SERVES 8 TO 10

HANDS-ON 15 MINUTES

TOTAL 50 MINUTES

1 medium-size long-necked butternut squash (about 2¼ pounds), peeled

2 tablespoons olive oil

2 teaspoons chopped fresh thyme

1 teaspoon kosher salt

¾ teaspoon black pepper

20 Bosc pear slices (from 1 [9-ounce] pear)

10 thin slices prosciutto (about 3 ounces), halved lengthwise

2 tablespoons balsamic glaze

❶ Preheat oven to 400°F. Cut neck from base of butternut squash; cut neck lengthwise into ¼-inch planks. Cut each plank into about 12 (2½- x 1-inch) pieces. Cut base of squash in half lengthwise; scoop out seeds. Cut base of squash into about 8 (2½- x 1-inch) pieces about ¼ inch thick. (You should have 20 pieces from base and neck.)

❷ Toss together squash pieces, olive oil, thyme, salt, and pepper in a large bowl. Spread in an even layer on a rimmed baking sheet, and bake in preheated oven until tender, about 18 minutes. Cool completely, about 15 minutes.

❸ Stack 1 squash piece and 1 pear slice; wrap with 1 prosciutto piece. Repeat with remaining squash pieces, pear slices, and prosciutto. Arrange parcels on a platter; drizzle with balsamic glaze.

MAKE IT YOURSELF

Can't find balsamic glaze? Make your own. It's delicious drizzled over a grilled steak or spooned over vanilla ice cream. Combine 1 cup balsamic vinegar and 2 tablespoons dark brown sugar in a small saucepan over low. Stir constantly until sugar dissolves, about 4 minutes. Boil over medium, stirring constantly, and reduce by a third until mixture coats the back of a spoon, 8 to 10 minutes. Be careful not to scorch.

Roasted Celery-Fennel Soup

This creamy soup gets a hint of sweetness from the caramelization of the vegetables. It's rich without filling you up.

SERVES 8 TO 10

HANDS-ON 30 MINUTES

TOTAL 1 HOUR

12   large celery stalks (about 2
      pounds), leaves reserved, stalks
      cut into 2-inch pieces
2   small fennel bulbs (about
      1¼ pounds), fronds reserved,
      bulb cut into 2-inch wedges
2   medium celery roots (about
      1¼ pounds), peeled and cut
      into 1-inch pieces
4   medium shallots (about 7
      ounces), halved
6   garlic cloves, peeled and
      smashed
6   tablespoons olive oil
2   teaspoons kosher salt
1   teaspoon black pepper
1   teaspoon fennel seeds
½   teaspoon celery seeds
5   cups chicken broth
1   cup heavy cream
⅔   cup crème fraîche
Fennel fronds, small celery leaves
      (optional)

❶ Preheat oven to 425°F, positioning racks in upper and lower thirds of oven. Toss together celery, fennel bulbs, celery roots, shallots, garlic, oil, salt, pepper, fennel seeds, and celery seeds in a large bowl. Divide mixture between 2 large rimmed baking sheets, and spread in an even layer. Bake in preheated oven until tender and browned, about 30 minutes, stirring once and switching pans top rack to bottom rack halfway through.

❷ Combine half of vegetables and half of chicken broth in a high-powered blender. Remove center piece of blender lid (to allow steam to escape); secure lid on blender, and place a clean towel over opening in lid. Process until smooth. Transfer processed mixture to a Dutch oven. Repeat with remaining vegetables and broth.

❸ Bring mixture to a simmer over medium, stirring occasionally. Stir in cream, and remove from heat. Top servings with crème fraîche. Garnish with fennel fronds and small celery leaves, if desired.

Note: You can make this soup ahead through Step 2. Cool and refrigerate, covered, up to 2 days. Reheat and stir in the cream before ladling into warm bowls and garnishing as in Step 3.

Kale-and-Escarole Salad with Parsnips and Dried Cranberries

Hearty winter greens become tender after a gentle massage with the dressing. This lovely salad is perfect for a large crowd. Substitute toasted pecans or hazelnuts for the cashews for a change of pace.

SERVES 8 TO 10

HANDS-ON 20 MINUTES

TOTAL 20 MINUTES

¼   cup sherry vinegar
1½   tablespoons pure maple syrup
1   tablespoon Dijon mustard
2   teaspoons chopped fresh
      rosemary
2   teaspoons minced garlic
1   teaspoon kosher salt
¾   teaspoon black pepper
½   cup extra-virgin olive oil
1   (1-pound) bunch curly kale,
      stems removed, leaves roughly
      chopped (about 10 cups)
2   cups shaved parsnips (about
      2 large parsnips)
1   (12-ounce) head escarole, roughly
      chopped (about 7 cups)
½   cup dried cranberries
½   cup chopped roasted, salted
      cashews

DECORATING TIP

Place settings frame the food and set the mood. Matchy-matchy is overrated. Mix and match sets of china for an easy, layered look. This homeowner's green and brown transferware, inherited and collected over time, gives the table a timeless look, but also sets a more casual tone. Collected pieces have a story to tell and are great conversation starters.

1 Stir together vinegar, maple syrup, mustard, rosemary, garlic, salt, and pepper in a small bowl. Add oil in a slow, steady stream, whisking constantly until smooth.

2 Combine kale and parsnips in a large bowl, and drizzle with ¼ cup of the dressing. Massage dressing into kale until tenderized and bright green, about 2 minutes. Add escarole and another ¼ cup of the dressing; toss to combine. Transfer to a platter, and sprinkle with dried cranberries and cashews. Serve with remaining dressing.

Brined and Blasted Turkey

Roasting the turkey in a scorching hot oven means it cooks in less time and the white meat stays moist and juicy.

SERVES 8 TO 10

HANDS-ON 30 MINUTES

TOTAL 17 HOURS, INCLUDING 12 HOURS CHILLING

2½ cups kosher salt
2½ gallons cold water
1   (12- to 15-pound) whole fresh turkey
1   stick (½ cup) butter, softened
1   tablespoon minced fresh rosemary leaves
1   tablespoon finely grated orange zest
2   teaspoons freshly ground black pepper
2   large onions
2   oranges
1   rosemary sprig
1 to 1½ cups chicken or turkey stock
½   cup white wine

1 Stir the salt and cold water together until the salt dissolves (no need to heat).

2 Remove the giblets and neck from the turkey; rinse with cold water. Transfer to a heavy-duty plastic garbage bag. Pour the salt water brine over the turkey in the bag. Knot the bag and refrigerate at least 12 or up to 24 hours. Remove the turkey from brine and drain cavity well; pat dry. Let the turkey come to room temperature.

3 Preheat oven to 450°F. Stir together the butter, rosemary, orange zest, and black pepper. Loosen and lift skin from turkey breast without totally detaching skin. Rub ¼ cup softened butter mixture under skin; replace skin.

4 Place turkey on a lightly greased roasting rack in a large roasting pan. Stuff the cavity of the bird with the onions, oranges, and rosemary. Tie ends of legs together with string; tuck wing tips under. Rub entire turkey with the remaining ¼ cup softened butter mixture. Roast the turkey at 450°F for 30 minutes. Baste the turkey with the pan juices and reduce heat to 400°F. Baste the turkey every 20 minutes for 2 to 2½ hours or until a meat thermometer inserted into thickest portion of thigh registers 145°F (the turkey will finish cooking as it rests). Shield with aluminum foil after 1 hour to prevent excessive browning, if necessary. Remove from oven, and let stand 30 minutes before carving.

5 Pour off all but 2 tablespoons fat and strain out any solids. Place the hot roasting pan over two burners and pour in the stock. Cook over medium, stirring to loosen browned bits from the bottom of the pan. Add the wine and bring to a boil, whisking constantly for 3 minutes. Taste and season with salt and pepper. Reduce further or add more stock to reach desired consistency.

Ginger-Rosemary Cranberry Sauce

Classic cranberry sauce gets an update with a bit of zesty warmth from fresh ginger and the distinctive pungency of woodsy rosemary.

MAKES 1½ CUPS

HANDS-ON 5 MINUTES

TOTAL 2 HOURS, 5 MINUTES

1   (12-ounce) package fresh cranberries
1   cup sugar
2   tablespoons finely grated orange zest
1   (1-inch) piece fresh ginger, peeled
1   teaspoon chopped fresh rosemary
Fresh rosemary, orange zest (optional)

Pulse cranberries and next 4 ingredients in a food processor until coarsely chopped. Transfer to a bowl; cover and chill 2 to 24 hours. Garnish with fresh rosemary and orange zest, if desired.

TIME-SAVER

No Harm, No Fowl: There's no fault in not cooking the holiday bird. In the South, local BBQ joints abound. Pick up a smoked turkey and serve it on a pretty platter with garnishes. No one has to know!

Creamed Swiss Chard with Zesty Walnut Topping

This is like an elevated creamed spinach with notes of citrus and brown butter.

SERVES 8 TO 10
HANDS-ON 45 MINUTES
TOTAL 45 MINUTES

6½ tablespoons salted butter
½   cup panko (Japanese-style breadcrumbs)
¼   cup walnut halves, finely chopped
½   teaspoon finely chopped fresh rosemary
¼   teaspoon crushed red pepper
½   teaspoon lemon zest
¼   teaspoon lime zest
1⅛ teaspoons kosher salt
4   (10-ounce) bunches Swiss chard, stems and leaves separated
½   cup finely chopped shallots (about 2 medium)
1   tablespoon minced garlic
3   tablespoons all-purpose flour
2   cups heavy cream
2   ounces Parmesan cheese, grated (about ½ cup)
½   teaspoon black pepper

❶ Melt 1½ tablespoons of the butter in a large skillet over medium-high. Cook until foaming subsides and butter begins to brown, about 4 minutes. Add panko, walnuts, rosemary, and red pepper; cook, stirring often, until toasted and fragrant, about 4 minutes. Remove from heat, and add lemon zest, lime zest, and ⅛ teaspoon of the salt. Set aside.

❷ Finely chop chard stems to equal 3 cups. (Discard remaining chard stems or reserve for another use.) Roughly chop chard leaves. Melt 2 tablespoons of the butter in a Dutch oven over medium-high. Add chard stems, shallots, and garlic, and cook, stirring often, until softened, about 6 minutes. Add chard leaves in batches, and cook, stirring until wilted after each addition, about 5 minutes. Transfer mixture to a colander, and drain, pressing lightly.

❸ Melt remaining 3 tablespoons butter in Dutch oven over medium. Sprinkle flour over butter, and cook, whisking constantly, until mixture is light golden brown, about 3 minutes. Slowly add cream, whisking constantly, and cook, whisking constantly, until thickened, about 3 minutes. Stir in cheese, pepper, and remaining 1 teaspoon salt; cook until cheese melts, about 1 minute. Stir drained chard into cream sauce. Top with walnut-panko mixture, and serve immediately.

FRESH IDEA

In many parts of the South we are blessed with mild winters, which means we are often able to entertain al fresco on occasion throughout the cooler season. If the temperature is comfortable, bring the holiday feast to the screened porch or patio for a more casual, family-style feel. Fresh-cut magnolia and evergreen branches arranged atop a weathered wood table and some candlelight are all you need to set the scene. If a chill is in the air, move the meal to a sunroom or enclosed porch for a similar easygoing farm feel.

Hasselback Potato Casserole with Comté and Bacon

Everybody loves a creamy potato gratin and this is a fun take on the classic. Be sure to choose various sizes of russet potatoes to make sure to fill the casserole dish. Substitute Gruyère for the Comté.

SERVES 8 TO 10
HANDS-ON 25 MINUTES
TOTAL 2 HOURS, 5 MINUTES

1   tablespoon salted butter, softened, for greasing dish
4   ounces Comté cheese, grated (about 1 cup)
4   ounces Grana Padano cheese or Parmigiano-Reggiano cheese, grated (about 1 cup)
2   cups heavy cream
8   bacon slices (about 8 ounces), cooked crisp and crumbled (about ½ cup)
2   tablespoons minced garlic
2   tablespoons chopped fresh thyme
2½ teaspoons kosher salt
1   teaspoon black pepper
6   pounds russet potatoes, peeled and cut into ⅛-inch-thick slices

❶ Preheat oven to 350°F. Grease a 3-quart oval baking dish with 1 tablespoon butter.

❷ Toss together cheeses in a large bowl. Remove and reserve ⅔ cup of cheese mixture in a small bowl.

❸ Stir cream, crumbled bacon, garlic, thyme, salt, and pepper into remaining cheese in large bowl. Add potato slices, and toss to coat well, separating slices as necessary to make sure all slices are coated.

4 Create stacks of potato slices (about 20 slices each); turn stacks on their side, and place stacks around perimeter of baking dish. Fill in center with remaining potato slices. (Potato slices should be very snug.) Pour remaining cream mixture from bowl over potatoes.

5 Cover with foil, and bake in preheated oven 30 minutes. Uncover and bake until top is pale golden, about 30 more minutes. Sprinkle with reserved cheese, and bake until deep golden brown and crisp, about 30 more minutes. Let stand 10 minutes before serving.

Whole Roasted Carrots with Honey and Herbs

Roasting brings out the inherent sweetness in carrots.

SERVES 8 TO 10
HANDS-ON 15 MINUTES
TOTAL 40 MINUTES

¼ cup plus 1 tablespoon (2½ ounces) salted butter
2 pounds medium carrots, peeled (about 18 carrots)
1½ teaspoons kosher salt
½ teaspoon black pepper
3 tablespoons honey
3 medium shallots, thinly sliced crosswise into rings (about 1 cup sliced)
2 tablespoons chopped fresh flat-leaf parsley
1½ tablespoons chopped fresh thyme
Fresh thyme leaves (optional)

1 Preheat oven to 400°F. Melt 2 tablespoons of the butter in a small saucepan over medium. Place carrots on a large rimmed baking sheet; drizzle with 2 tablespoons melted butter, and sprinkle with salt and pepper. Toss to coat. Bake in preheated oven 20 minutes, stirring once halfway through.

2 Meanwhile, combine honey and remaining 3 tablespoons butter in same small saucepan. Cook over medium, stirring constantly, until butter is melted and mixture begins to bubble. Add shallots, separating rings, and cook, stirring often, until slightly softened, 1 to 2 minutes. Remove from heat, and stir in parsley and chopped thyme. Spoon mixture over partially baked carrots, and stir gently to coat carrots. Return carrots to oven, and bake until carrots and shallots are tender and caramelized, about 15 minutes, stirring once halfway through. Garnish with fresh thyme leaves, if desired.

VINTAGE VIGNETTE

Enlist everyday items into service in uncommon ways. An old, enameled-steel egg carrier becomes a resting place for ornaments, plants, and posies, morphing into an interesting focal point for a side table laden with parting favors wrapped with pretty paper and velvet ribbon. The flicker of candlelight and thoughtful accents turn the most utilitarian of pieces into an unexpected still life sure to capture the attention of dinner party guests.

Deep-Dish Apple-Sweet Potato Pie with Maple Ice Cream

This warm-spiced pie is a stunning end to an elegant meal thanks to the mosaic of sweet potato and apple slices surrounded by a flaky, fluted crust. Maple ice cream takes this to a whole 'nother level.

SERVES 8 TO 10

HANDS-ON 40 MINUTES

TOTAL 19 HOURS, 5 MINUTES

CRUST

3¾ cups (about 16 ounces) all-purpose flour

1½ teaspoons table salt

1¼ cups (10 ounces) cold unsalted butter, cut into ½-inch pieces

10 to 11 tablespoons ice water

FILLING

1½ pounds Granny Smith apples (about 3 medium), peeled and cut into ¼-inch-thick slices (about 4 cups)

2 pounds Fuji apples (about 4 medium), peeled and cut into ¼-inch-thick slices (about 5½ cups)

1¼ pounds sweet potatoes (about 1½ medium), peeled and cut into ⅛-inch-thick half-moons (about 5 cups)

6 tablespoons cornstarch

2 tablespoons fresh lemon juice

2 teaspoons ground cinnamon

1 cup plus 2 tablespoons granulated sugar

1 large egg, beaten

ADDITIONAL INGREDIENT

Maple Ice Cream (page 29)

1 Prepare the Crust: Pulse flour and salt in a food processor until blended, about 3 times. Add butter pieces, and lightly toss to coat with flour. Pulse until the butter is the size of peas, 5 or 6 times. Gradually add 10 tablespoons of the water, and pulse just until the dough begins to clump together. Add up to 1 tablespoon water, 1 teaspoon at a time, if needed. (Do not let dough form a ball.) Turn dough out onto work surface. Gently gather about two-thirds of dough, and shape into a flat disk. Shape remaining dough into a second flat disk. Wrap each disk in plastic wrap, and chill 1 to 24 hours.

2 Preheat oven to 425°F. Lightly grease a 10- x 2-inch deep-dish fluted tart pan with removable bottom, and place on a large, parchment paper-lined rimmed baking sheet.

3 Place largest dough disk on lightly floured surface, and roll into a 15-inch circle. Fit into prepared tart pan, pressing into bottom and up sides of pan and allowing excess to drape over edges. Roll smaller dough portion into a 12-inch circle; place on a parchment paper-lined baking sheet. Chill both piecrusts while preparing filling.

4 Prepare the Filling: Stir together apples, sweet potatoes, cornstarch, lemon juice, cinnamon, and 1 cup of the sugar in a large bowl. Spoon the filling into prepared bottom crust, mounding filling and making sure there are minimal air pockets. Brush edges of bottom crust with a small amount of beaten egg. Place top crust over filling, pressing edges of top and bottom crusts to seal. Trim edges, leaving ¾ inch overhanging. Fold edges under and crimp, pressing upward so as not to seal crust to tart pan. (This will help to more easily remove pie from pan.) Brush top crust with remaining beaten egg; sprinkle with remaining

2 tablespoons sugar. Cut 5 slits in center of crust to allow steam to escape.

5 Bake in preheated oven on lowest oven rack 15 minutes. Reduce oven temperature to 375°F; continue baking until pie is deep golden brown and sweet potatoes and apples are tender, about 1 hour to 1 hour 10 minutes, shielding pie with aluminum foil as needed to prevent excessive browning. Cool pie completely on baking sheet on a wire rack, about 4 hours.

6 To remove pie from tart pan, place hand underneath pie in center of removable bottom. Using opposite hand, gradually release top crust from edge of pan while rotating pie and pressing up lightly from beneath pie. Once side of tart pan has been released, slide pie from bottom of pan onto serving plate. Serve with Maple Ice Cream.

MAPLE ICE CREAM

1¼ cups heavy cream
1¼ cups whole milk
1 teaspoon kosher salt
¾ cup Grade B maple syrup
6 large egg yolks

1 Stir together cream, milk, salt, and ½ cup of the maple syrup in a medium saucepan. Cook over medium, stirring often, until mixture is steaming and edges are foaming, about 6 minutes.

2 Whisk together egg yolks and remaining ¼ cup maple syrup in a medium bowl. Fill a large bowl halfway with ice, and set aside.

3 Gradually whisk ½ cup hot cream mixture into egg mixture. Repeat with another ½ cup cream mixture. Gradually whisk egg mixture into remaining cream mixture, and cook over medium, stirring constantly, until mixture coats the back of a spoon, 3 to 4 minutes. Transfer

to a large bowl, and place in ice bath. Let stand in ice bath, stirring occasionally, until completely cool, about 30 minutes. Cover and chill 8 to 12 hours.

4 Pour mixture into frozen freezer bowl of a 1½-quart electric ice-cream maker, and proceed according to manufacturer's instructions. (Instructions and times may vary.) Transfer to an airtight freezer-safe container; freeze until firm, about 3 hours. Makes 1 quart

TIME-SAVER

Make the ice cream up to 1 week in advance and freeze. Make the pie dough up to 24 hours in advance and refrigerate.

CHRISTMAS
at the lake

A relaxing weekend retreat is the favored family spot for fireside feasts. This one is inspired by wood smoke and cool-season ingredients with decorations that celebrate the surroundings.

THE MENU
serves 4 to 6

RED PEPPER-BOURBON
TODDY

BEANS AND GREENS WREATH

PROSCIUTTO CUPS
WITH OLIVE, PEPPER,
AND ONION RELISH

ROASTED BEETS WITH
HAZELNUTS AND
POMEGRANATE-SHERRY
REDUCTION

SMOKED PORK
TENDERLOINS WITH
SHERRY MUSHROOM SAUCE

BAKED SWEET POTATOES
WITH MAPLE AND THYME
CRÈME FRAÎCHE

SMOKED CABBAGE WITH
CORIANDER AND PARSLEY-
LEMON BROWN BUTTER

SALTED CARAMEL
APPLE BREAD PUDDING
WITH IRISH WHISKEY
WHIPPED CREAM

DECK THE DECK

Mild Southern temperatures allow doors to be flung open and drinks to be enjoyed on the deck while taking in the lake view. A self-serve bar just inside takes stress off the host.

OUTFIT THE ENTRY

A long trestle table gets gussied up for the season with greenery, gifts, and ornaments—all with a nod to outdoors.

CATCH THE SPIRIT

Decorations inspired by weekends at the lake make new uses for fishing creels, nets, old oars, rusty planter boxes, and vintage signs and dishes. Embellishing items from your surroundings lets you see them in a new light and creates an inviting holiday look grounded in a sense of place. Mini creel ornaments can be called into service to hold favors, place cards, or posies of greenery and berries. Larger ones might hold a centerpiece or gifts for guests to take home as the party ends. Yellow and red ball flowers, known as Craspedia, add a graphic, bright note to traditional arrangements of pine, fir, and spruce.

Clockwise from top: Prosciutto Cups with Olive, Pepper, and Onion Relish; Beans and Greens Wreath; Red Pepper-Bourbon Toddy

FIRESIDE SUPPER

Setting a casual table next to a roaring fire creates a warm, comforting vibe that begs guests to linger.

Smoked Pork Tenderloins
with Sherry Mushroom Sauce

Roasted Beets with Hazelnuts and Pomegranate-Sherry
Reduction, Baked Sweet Potatoes with Maple and Thyme
Crème Fraîche, Smoked Cabbage with Coriander and
Parsley-Lemon Brown Butter

Salted Caramel Apple Bread Pudding
with Irish Whiskey Whipped Cream

Red Pepper-Bourbon Toddy

By combining the cocktail ingredients without ice, you can make the cocktails to order for your guests.

SERVES 6
HANDS-ON 10 MINUTES
TOTAL 10 MINUTES

1¼ cups (10 ounces) bourbon
¼ cup (2 ounces) Cointreau
⅓ cup red pepper jelly
¾ cup plus 2 tablespoons fresh lemon juice (from 5 lemons)
2 tablespoons kosher salt
2 tablespoons granulated sugar

1 Combine bourbon, Cointreau, pepper jelly, and ¾ cup of the lemon juice in a medium pitcher, and stir until pepper jelly is completely dissolved.

2 Place remaining 2 tablespoons lemon juice in a shallow saucer. Combine kosher salt and sugar in a separate small saucer, and stir to blend. Prepare chilled cocktail glasses by dipping rims in lemon juice and then in salt-sugar mixture to coat rims. Place 1 ice cube in each prepared glass.

3 Fill a cocktail shaker with ice and about ½ cup of mixture per serving. Shake vigorously until thoroughly chilled and ice crystals have broken up, about 30 seconds. Strain mixture into prepared glass.

Beans and Greens Wreath

Both eye-catching and taste bud-satisfying, this festive appetizer wreath looks its holiday best when some of the green and red filling shows through.

SERVES 6
HANDS-ON 20 MINUTES
TOTAL 45 MINUTES

4 ounces spicy pork sausage
¼ cup diced red bell pepper
¼ cup diced yellow onion
1 (10-ounce) package frozen spinach, thawed and drained
8 ounces cream cheese, softened
6 ounces Monterey Jack cheese, shredded (about 1½ cups)
½ cup drained and rinsed canned black-eyed peas
2 (10-ounce) cans refrigerated crescent roll dough

1 Cook sausage in a large nonstick skillet over medium-high, stirring to break up sausage, until browned, about 6 minutes. Remove sausage from skillet to a plate lined with paper towels, reserving drippings in skillet. Add red bell pepper and onion to skillet, and cook until pepper and onion are slightly softened, about 5 minutes. Remove to another plate lined with paper towels to drain. Squeeze thawed and drained spinach with paper towels until you have removed all moisture and spinach is very dry.

2 Stir together cream cheese and Monterey Jack cheese in a medium bowl. Add cooked sausage, pepper, onion, and spinach. Gently fold in black-eyed peas; stir to combine.

3 Separate crescent roll dough into triangles. Line a baking sheet with parchment paper. Arrange dough triangles in a ring on parchment so the short sides of the triangles form a 4-inch circle in the center. The dough triangles will overlap a bit, and the tips of the triangles will hang over the edges of the baking sheet. The dough will look like a sunburst.

4 Spoon sausage mixture in the part of the dough circle closest to the center of the ring. Bring each dough triangle tip up and over the filling, tucking the dough tip under the bottom of the center of the dough circle in the inside to secure. When finished, the dough ring should look like a striped wreath. Chill until ready to bake.

5 Preheat oven to 375ºF, with 1 rack in the bottom third of the oven. Place a baking sheet in preheated oven for 10 minutes. Slide wreath on parchment paper to preheated baking sheet, and bake until the dough is fully cooked and golden brown, about 20 minutes. Cool a few minutes before sliding entire wreath onto a round platter and slicing into portions. Serve hot.

TIME-SAVER

Make the filling ahead of time and chill. When ready to assemble, take filling out of the refrigerator and let soften so you can spoon it in the dough, wrap, and bake.

Prosciutto Cups with Olive, Pepper, and Onion Relish

Prosciutto crisps up in the oven to form the perfect cup for other favorites of the antipasti platter. Substitute pancetta or salami for the prosciutto if you like.

SERVES 5

HANDS-ON 20 MINUTES

TOTAL 30 MINUTES

3   ounces presliced prosciutto (about 10 slices)
¼   cup chopped pitted Castelvetrano olives
¼   cup chopped drained Peppadew peppers
¼   cup chopped drained marinated cipollini onions
½   tablespoon balsamic glaze (page 23)

1 Preheat oven to 375°F. Cut prosciutto slices in half crosswise, and fit 1 piece into bottom and sides of each of 20 cups of a 24-cup miniature muffin pan. Bake in preheated oven until the fat in the prosciutto has turned golden and the meat has started to crisp, about 10 minutes. Remove from oven, and place on a plate lined with paper towels; cool. (Prosciutto will crisp further upon cooling.)

2 Finely chop olives, peppers, and onions, and stir to combine. Spoon about ½ teaspoon relish into each cooled prosciutto cup, and place cups on a platter. Drizzle balsamic glaze over cups.

Roasted Beets with Hazelnuts and Pomegranate-Sherry Reduction

Using a mix of ruby red beets and sweet golden beets adds colorful interest to this earthy salad-meets-side dish. The tender leaves of the beet tops get wilted and tossed in the mix, so nothing is wasted.

SERVES 4

HANDS-ON 20 MINUTES

TOTAL 2 HOURS, 20 MINUTES

1   bunch medium-size red beets with tender leaves
1   bunch medium-size golden beets with tender leaves
¼   cup extra-virgin olive oil
1½ teaspoons kosher salt
¾   teaspoon black pepper
3   tablespoons sorghum syrup
¼   cup high-quality sherry vinegar
½   cup refrigerated pomegranate juice
¼   cup vegetable stock
2   large shallots, halved and thinly sliced (about 1 cup slices)
⅓   cup chopped toasted hazelnuts

1 Preheat oven to 375°F. Trim beet stems and greens from roots; wash beet greens well, and pat dry. Roughly chop beet greens and all tender stems, discarding any tougher leaves or stems. (You should have about 4 to 5 cups of chopped leaves.) Scrub beets well. Toss together whole beets, 2 tablespoons of the olive oil, 1 teaspoon of the salt, and ½ teaspoon of the pepper. Place beets in a roasting pan, and cover with aluminum foil.

2 Bake in preheated oven until tender when pierced with a knife, about 1 hour and 15 minutes. Cool 1 hour. Peel and trim whole beets, and cut into ¼-inch wedges.

3 Place sorghum in a small saucepan over medium. Bring sorghum to a simmer, whisking often, until small bubbles appear over entire surface and it becomes very thick but not burned, about 30 seconds. Slowly add sherry vinegar, pomegranate juice, and vegetable stock, whisking to combine. Bring mixture to a boil, cooking without stirring until mixture is reduced to a syrupy consistency and measures about ⅓ cup, about 15 minutes.

4 Just before serving, heat remaining 2 tablespoons olive oil in a large skillet over medium-high. Add shallots, and cook until beginning to soften, about 3 minutes. Add reserved chopped beet greens and remaining ½ teaspoon salt and ¼ teaspoon pepper, and cook, stirring often, until shallots are golden brown and beet greens are wilted and tender. Toss mixture with cooked beets. Drizzle with pomegranate-sherry syrup, and sprinkle with hazelnuts.

TIME-SAVER
In a pinch, fill prosciutto cups with Italian jarred pickled vegetables, or "giardiniera." Drain first so cups don't get soggy.

Smoked Pork Tenderloins with Sherry Mushroom Sauce

You could use your smoker to smoke these pork tenderloins and the Smoked Cabbage in this chapter at the same time.

SERVES 6

HANDS-ON 50 MINUTES

TOTAL 11 HOURS, INCLUDING 8 HOURS CHILLING

PORK

2 pork tenderloins (about 2 pounds)

BRINE

2 tablespoons kosher salt

3 garlic cloves, peeled and smashed

5 black peppercorns, cracked

2 thyme sprigs

3 cups apple cider

RUB

2 tablespoons dry mustard

½ tablespoon onion powder

½ tablespoon garlic powder

½ tablespoon ground coriander

1 teaspoon black pepper

ADDITIONAL INGREDIENT

3 large applewood chunks, soaked in water to cover 1 hour

SAUCE

2 tablespoons olive oil

1 pound sliced cremini mushrooms

⅔ cup dry sherry

1 tablespoon chopped fresh thyme leaves

½ teaspoon kosher salt

¼ teaspoon black pepper

3 tablespoons heavy cream

2 tablespoons chopped fresh flat-leaf parsley

❶ Prepare the Pork: Remove pork tenderloins from wrapper; rinse and pat dry. Place on work surface, and trim any silver skin. Trim small, thinner ends, leaving tenderloin pieces that are uniform in thickness from end to end.

❷ Prepare the Brine: Stir together salt, garlic cloves, peppercorns, thyme sprigs, and 1½ cups apple cider in a medium saucepan over medium. Warm gently, stirring just until salt is dissolved, about 3 minutes. Remove from heat, and stir in remaining 1½ cups apple cider. Remove and reserve ¼ cup of the brine liquid.

❸ Place tenderloins in a ziplock plastic bag, and pour remaining brine with solids into bag, making sure all pieces of pork are submerged. Seal bag, and chill 8 hours or overnight. Remove pork from brine; rinse with cold water, and pat dry. Discard brine. Tie tenderloins at intervals with kitchen twine so they are round and of even thickness from end to end.

❹ Prepare the Rub: Stir together dry mustard, onion powder, garlic, powder, ground coriander, and black pepper in a small bowl. Rub mixture evenly over pork, and let stand at room temperature 30 minutes.

❺ Prepare smoker according to manufacturer's instructions, bringing internal temperature to 225°F; maintain temperature 20 minutes. Smoke tenderloins on the top rack of the smoker 1 hour, maintaining internal temperature at 225°F and basting pork twice with reserved ¼ cup brine. Add soaked applewood chunks to the wood reservoir. Continue to smoke pork until a thermometer registers 140°F to 142°F when inserted in thickest portion of pork, about 1 more hour, maintaining internal temperature at 225°F and basting pork twice with reserved brine. Remove pork from smoker, and let stand 10 minutes before removing twine and slicing.

❻ While pork cooks, prepare the Sauce: Heat oil in a large skillet over medium-high; add mushrooms, and cook, stirring occasionally, until mushrooms are tender and liquid has completely evaporated, about 12 minutes. Stir in sherry, thyme, salt, and pepper; simmer until sherry has reduced by half, about 6 minutes. Stir in heavy cream, and cook until sauce has thickened slightly, 2 to 3 minutes. Remove from heat, and stir in parsley. Serve with pork.

SPANISH SHERRY

Sherry is a fortified wine from Spain that ranges in color from gold to brown, and in flavor from bone dry to very sweet. Finos are considered dry and light, while olorosos are sweet, dark, and robust. Sherry is often used in cooking but may also be consumed as an aperitif or after-dinner drink. Dry sherry is usually served chilled and sweet sherry is served at room temperature.

Baked Sweet Potatoes with Maple and Thyme Crème Fraîche

Sweet and savory come together in one tender creamy sweet potato topped with a luxurious crème fraîche laced with sweet maple syrup and fresh burst of savory herbs. The crème fraîche will melt and spill out of the sweet potato if it's added right after they come out of the oven.

SERVES 6

HANDS-ON 10 MINUTES

TOTAL 1 HOUR, 10 MINUTES

6   (6-ounce) sweet potatoes

¾   cup crème fraîche

1   tablespoon maple syrup

2   teaspoons fresh thyme leaves

2   teaspoons finely chopped fresh flat-leaf parsley

3   tablespoons salted butter

1½   teaspoons flaked sea salt

1   teaspoon coarsely ground black pepper

❶ Preheat oven to 375°F. Pierce sweet potatoes several times with a fork. Place sweet potatoes a few inches apart on a baking sheet. Bake in preheated oven until tender when pierced with a knife, about 1 hour.

❷ Meanwhile, stir together crème fraîche, maple syrup, thyme, and parsley in a small bowl.

❸ Cut a lengthwise slit in each sweet potato, and press on sides to open up. Dollop each potato with ½ tablespoon butter and about 2 tablespoons crème fraîche mixture. Sprinkle evenly with sea salt and pepper.

Smoked Cabbage with Coriander and Parsley-Lemon Brown Butter

The light smoke flavor is enhanced by the bright lemon and coriander flavors in the nutty brown butter. The idea is to put the cabbages in the smoker while the pork tenderloins smoke. If you aren't using the smoker for the pork, boil the cabbages for 1 hour and prepare through Step 4. Let the cabbages steam in the foil while you get the rest of the meal ready, then proceed with Steps 6 and 7.

SERVES 6

HANDS-ON 30 MINUTES

TOTAL 3 HOURS, 30 MINUTES

2   (3-pound) cabbages, outer leaves removed

4 to 5 large applewood chunks, soaked in water for 1 hour

½   teaspoon black pepper

1¼   teaspoons kosher salt

1½   cups (12 ounces) unsalted butter

1   lemon, peeled, sectioned, and chopped (about 1 tablespoon)

1   tablespoon chopped fresh flat-leaf parsley

½   teaspoon ground coriander

❶ Place cabbages in a large stockpot, and add enough water to cover cabbages completely. Bring to a boil over high. Boil until cabbages are slightly tender and yield when pierced with a knife, about 30 minutes.

❷ Remove cabbages from water to a work surface lined with a towel to absorb draining water; let cool. Use a paring knife to remove core from each cabbage, leaving the rest of the cabbage whole. Cool for 30 minutes.

❸ Prepare smoker according to manufacturer's instructions, using a low cooking grate and a water pan. Place soaked wood chunks on hot coals or in wood reservoir, and bring internal temperature to 225°F. Maintain temperature 20 minutes.

❹ Place each cabbage in the middle of a large piece of heavy-duty aluminum foil, cored side up. Sprinkle inside of each cabbage with ¼ teaspoon pepper and ½ teaspoon of the salt. Gently insert ½ cup butter (1 stick) into each cored space. Wrap each cabbage tightly in foil.

❺ Place wrapped cabbages on low cooking grate, cored side up so butter remains inside, and smoke until cabbages are very tender but still maintain their shape, about 2 hours, maintaining internal temperature at 225°F.

❻ Place remaining ½ cup butter in a saucepan over medium-low, and cook until butter is brown and fragrant, about 6 minutes. Transfer brown butter to a medium bowl, and set over a bowl of ice water. Stir butter until it reaches a smooth, creamy consistency, about 5 minutes. Stir in chopped lemon sections, parsley, coriander, and remaining ¼ teaspoon salt.

❼ To serve, unwrap cabbages, and cut each into 6 wedges. Top each wedge with a generous spoonful of browned butter mixture.

HOLIDAY HELPER

If you're firing up the smoker for one recipe, take advantage of it for another. Soak shelled pecans in water 10 minutes; drain. Place in an aluminum pan on the smoker for 30 minutes. Perfect for giving!

Salted Caramel Apple Bread Pudding with Irish Whiskey Whipped Cream

This classic bread pudding is rich and moist with a crunchy top and edges. Spiced apples and boozy whipped cream take it over the top.

SERVES 6

HANDS-ON 15 MINUTES

TOTAL 2 HOURS, 5 MINUTES

- 1 (1-pound) brioche loaf, cut into 1-inch cubes (about 12 cups)
- 4 large eggs, beaten
- 2 cups half-and-half
- 1 cup whole milk
- 1 teaspoon vanilla extract
- 1 cup granulated sugar
- 6 tablespoons salted butter
- 2 large Granny Smith apples, peeled and cubed
- ¼ teaspoon ground cinnamon
- ¼ teaspoon ground nutmeg
- 1 cup whipping cream
- 2 tablespoons Irish whiskey
- 2 tablespoons powdered sugar
- Salted caramel sauce (such as Smucker's Simple Delight Salted Caramel Topping)

❶ Preheat oven to 350°F. Spread bread cubes in an even layer on a large rimmed baking sheet. Bake in preheated oven until light golden brown, about 15 minutes, stirring once. Set aside.

❷ Whisk together eggs, half-and-half, milk, vanilla, and ¾ cup of the granulated sugar in a large bowl. Set aside.

ARRANGEMENTS

Easy centerpieces can be made using clippings from your surroundings, such as longleaf pine, holly, or cedar. Save the bottom branches that were cut from the Christmas tree to accommodate the tree stand. Add in a few bright spots from the flower market or grocery store: berries, flowers, fruit, nuts, even herbs make great filler.

❸ Melt butter in a large skillet over medium, and cook, stirring often, until browned and fragrant, about 5 minutes. Transfer butter to a small bowl. (Do not wipe skillet clean.)

❹ Add apples, cinnamon, nutmeg, and remaining ¼ cup granulated sugar to skillet. Cook until sugar melts and apples begin to soften, about 3 minutes. Stir 3 tablespoons of the brown butter into apple mixture, and cook until juices become syrupy, 3 to 4 minutes. Remove from heat, and cool 20 minutes.

❺ Add apple mixture and toasted brioche cubes to egg mixture, and toss gently to combine. Let stand 10 minutes.

❻ Grease a 13- x 9-inch baking dish with 1 tablespoon of the brown butter; spoon the soaked brioche-and-apple mixture into the baking dish, and drizzle with remaining 2 tablespoons brown butter.

❼ Bake in preheated oven until mixture is puffed, set, and golden brown on top, 45 to 50 minutes. Let stand 10 minutes before serving.

❽ Meanwhile, place whipping cream, whiskey, and powdered sugar in a small chilled bowl. Beat with an electric mixer on high speed until soft peaks form.

❾ Serve warm bread pudding with whipped cream and salted caramel sauce.

CHRISTMAS
in the mountains

Selecting or cutting the perfect tree is a long-standing holiday tradition. Fortify your troops for the hunt and the tree decorating ahead with an easy, hearty woodland feast.

THE MENU
serves 8

SPICED HOT CIDER

CARAMELIZED ONION-
BACON DIP

TARRAGON AND MUSTARD
PICKLED CRAWFISH TAILS

DUCK GUMBO

HERBED YEAST SPOON ROLLS

MIXED GREENS AND
SPINACH SALAD
WITH MAPLE-CIDER
VINAIGRETTE

SPICED GINGERBREAD LATTE

CARAMELIZED
APPLE CANNOLI WITH
PRALINE SAUCE

HOLIDAY WELCOME

*A grand entry decked out in wreaths, ribbon, and a dense garland
of evergreen boughs and brass bells greets guests.*

LIGHT THE WAY

After the tree is cut, lantern light guides guests indoors to mingle, raise glasses, and gather together at the table.

PATIO AND PORCH

Festive vignettes beckon at every turn. A table on the porch combines rustic elements from outdoors and in.

Spiced Hot Cider

COMFORT AND JOY

Lumberjack plaids, denim, and copper add color and glow to organic elements like wool, wood, stone, and pine. A strip of bright wool plaid outfits a bear carving at the entry while the antlers of tiny reindeer, wrapped in spun wool, hold place cards for the table. Hints of flora and fauna are all that's needed to drive home the mountain holiday theme in this cabin setting. A slice from a fallen tree becomes a wreath over a mantel decked with traditional stockings and greenery.

Tarragon and Mustard Pickled Crawfish Tails, Caramelized Onion-Bacon Dip

Mixed Greens and Spinach Salad
with Maple-Cider Vinaigrette,
Herbed Yeast Spoon Rolls

Duck Gumbo

Spiced Gingerbread Latte,
Caramelized Apple Cannoli
with Praline Sauce

Spiced Hot Cider

A perfect holiday revitalizer, served as is or spiked as in the boozy variation, that can be made ahead up to several days.

SERVES 8

HANDS-ON 30 MINUTES

TOTAL 30 MINUTES

2   quarts apple cider
3   (3-inch) cinnamon sticks
1   (2- x 1-inch) piece peeled fresh
    ginger (about 1¾ ounces)
2   (2-inch) orange peel strips
2   (2-inch) lemon peel strips
4   allspice berries
10 whole cloves
10 whole black peppercorns
Cinnamon sticks, lemon or orange
    slices (optional)

❶ Bring cider, cinnamon sticks, ginger, orange peel, lemon peel, allspice berries, cloves, and peppercorns to a boil in a large saucepan over medium-high, stirring occasionally; reduce heat to medium-low, and simmer 15 minutes.

❷ Pour liquid through a fine wire-mesh strainer into a pitcher; discard solids. Garnish with cinnamon sticks and lemon or orange slices, if desired.

Boozy Spiced Hot Cider: Prepare cider as directed, stirring in 1 cup bourbon, applejack, rum, or brandy after simmering.

Caramelized Onion-Bacon Dip

Serve this simple but flavorful dip with assorted crackers, sliced vegetables, gourmet potato chips, or toasted baguette slices.

SERVES 32

HANDS-ON 43 MINUTES

TOTAL 53 MINUTES

8   bacon slices
3   large Vidalia or other sweet
     onions, halved and coarsely
     chopped
½   teaspoon kosher salt
2   tablespoons sherry vinegar
1   teaspoon finely chopped fresh
     thyme
1¼   cups sour cream
1   cup mayonnaise
¼   teaspoon black pepper
Crumbled bacon, thyme sprigs
     (optional)

❶ Cook bacon in a large skillet over medium until crisp, 8 to 10 minutes. Drain on paper towels; reserve 3 tablespoons drippings in skillet. Crumble bacon, and set aside.

❷ Add onions and salt to drippings in skillet; cook over medium-high, stirring occasionally, until onions soften and just begin to turn golden, 8 to 10 minutes. Reduce heat to medium, and cook, stirring often, until onions turn deep golden brown, 20 to 25 minutes. Stir in vinegar, stirring to loosen browned bits from bottom of skillet. Cook,

stirring often, until vinegar has almost evaporated. Stir in thyme. Transfer mixture to a large bowl; cool 10 minutes.

❸ Add sour cream, mayonnaise, and pepper to onion mixture in bowl; stir to combine. Fold in crumbled bacon. Spoon into a serving dish. Garnish with additional crumbled bacon and thyme, if desired.

Hot Caramelized Onion-Bacon Dip:
Stir ½ cup Parmesan cheese into the dip and spread in a casserole dish; bake at 350°F for 20 minutes.

HOLIDAY HELPER

Top 5 Appetizer Tips

1. No chafing dish for warm items? A fondue pot or slow cooker are good stand-ins.

2. Plan to have both hot and cold appetizers that guests can easily serve themselves.

3. Don't freeze items that contain raw or hard-cooked eggs, mayonnaise, or raw veggies.

4. If appetizers are all you're serving, plan on 6 to 8 servings per guest. If a meal follows, count on 2 to 4 appetizer servings per guest.

5. Firm foods can be used as creative containers for dips. Spoon dips into a hollowed-out pineapple, bell pepper, or rustic bread loaf.

Tarragon and Mustard Pickled Crawfish Tails

If you love traditional Southern pickled shrimp, you'll love this bayou take on that classic. If using raw crawfish, undercook a bit so they don't become rubbery when pickled.

SERVES 8

HANDS-ON 12 MINUTES

TOTAL 8 HOURS, 12 MINUTES, INCLUDING 8 HOURS CHILLING

2   pounds peeled cooked crawfish tails
1   small sweet onion, halved and sliced
4   thyme sprigs
3   garlic cloves, halved
3   bay leaves
1   cup olive oil
1   cup tarragon vinegar
⅓   cup drained capers
3   tablespoons Dijon or coarse-grain mustard
2   tablespoons chopped fresh flat-leaf parsley
2   tablespoons chopped fresh tarragon
1½   teaspoons kosher salt
1   teaspoon black pepper

Toss together crawfish, onion, thyme, garlic, and bay leaves in a large airtight container. Whisk together oil, vinegar, capers, mustard, parsley, tarragon, salt, and pepper; pour over crawfish mixture. Cover and chill 8 hours, stirring occasionally. Remove and discard thyme sprigs and bay leaves. Serve with a slotted spoon.

Duck Gumbo

A dark roux adds nuttiness to this rich, hearty gumbo. For a pretty presentation, reserve a cooked duck breast. Slice the breast and arrange a few slices on top of each serving before garnishing.

SERVES 8

HANDS-ON 1 HOUR, 19 MINUTES

TOTAL 2 HOURS, 4 MINUTES

4   boneless duck breasts (about 1 pound 5 ounces)
3   tablespoons salted butter
½   teaspoon kosher salt
½   teaspoon black pepper
1½   pounds Conecuh sausage, sliced
½   cup (about 2 ⅛ ounces) all-purpose flour
1½   cups chopped onion (from 1 large onion)
1   cup chopped green bell pepper (from 1 bell pepper)
3   celery stalks, chopped
2   garlic cloves, minced
2   tablespoons Cajun seasoning
2   bay leaves
6   cups chicken broth
1   (14.5-ounce) can diced tomatoes, undrained
1   tablespoon Worcestershire sauce
Hot cooked rice
Chopped scallions, hot pepper sauce (optional)

❶ Place duck breasts between 2 sheets of plastic wrap. Pound lightly to even thickness, if necessary, about ½ to ¾ inch. Discard plastic wrap. Using a sharp knife, score skin in a ¾-inch diamond pattern (do not cut into flesh).

❷ Melt 2 tablespoons of the butter in a large Dutch oven over medium-high. Sprinkle duck with salt and pepper. Add duck to pan, skin side down, and cook until skin is browned and crisp, about 5 minutes. Turn duck breasts over, reduce heat to medium, and cook 2 minutes. Remove duck from Dutch oven, reserving drippings in Dutch oven. Cool duck 5 minutes; remove and discard skin. Cut duck into ½-inch pieces. Keep warm.

❸ Cook sausage in duck drippings over medium-high until browned on both sides, about 10 minutes. Remove with a slotted spoon, reserving drippings in Dutch oven; set aside, and keep warm.

❹ Add remaining 1 tablespoon butter to Dutch oven to equal ½ cup butter and drippings. Add flour, stirring constantly. Cook over medium, stirring constantly with a flat-bottomed wooden spoon to loosen browned bits from bottom of Dutch oven, until deep brown, 35 to 40 minutes. Add onion, bell pepper, celery, and garlic; cook until vegetables are tender, about 6 minutes. Add Cajun seasoning and bay leaves; cook 2 minutes. Gradually whisk in broth. Stir in tomatoes, Worcestershire sauce, duck, and sausage. Bring to a boil. Cover, reduce heat to low, and simmer until duck is tender, 30 to 45 minutes.

❺ Discard bay leaves. Serve gumbo over rice. Serve with scallions and hot pepper sauce, if desired.

HOLIDAY HELPER

Transfer the gumbo to a slow cooker set to WARM to safely keep the main course hot while the crowd is out cutting the perfect tree.

Herbed Yeast Spoon Rolls

This bread batter can be made up to 1 week in advance; just keep it covered well in the refrigerator until you're ready to make the rolls. Feel free to leave out the herbs if you'd like plain rolls to go with your meal.

SERVES 20

HANDS-ON 14 MINUTES

TOTAL 4 HOURS, 34 MINUTES, INCLUDING 4 HOURS CHILLING

2   cups lukewarm water (100°F to 110°F)
1   (¼-ounce) envelope active dry yeast
¼   cup plus 1 teaspoon granulated sugar
4   cups (about 16 ounces) self-rising flour
¾   cup (6 ounces) salted butter, melted and cooled
1   large egg, lightly beaten
2   teaspoons chopped fresh chives
2   teaspoons chopped fresh flat-leaf parsley
1   teaspoon chopped garlic
½   teaspoon kosher salt

1 Combine lukewarm water, yeast, and 1 teaspoon of the sugar in a large bowl; let stand 5 minutes. Stir together flour, butter, egg, chives, parsley, garlic, salt, and remaining ¼ cup sugar. Add to yeast mixture, and stir until blended. Spoon batter into 20 greased muffin cups, filling ¾ full. Chill 4 hours or overnight.

2 Preheat oven to 350°F. Bake until rolls are golden, about 20 minutes.

Mixed Greens and Spinach Salad with Maple-Cider Vinaigrette

The candied almonds here are a game changer—adding delicious, crunchy sweetness to this green salad, dotted with red accents. Substitute dried cranberries for the cherries and feta for the crumbled goat cheese for a change of pace.

SERVES 8

HANDS-ON 20 MINUTES

TOTAL 20 MINUTES

1   tablespoon salted butter
½   cup sliced almonds
2   tablespoons granulated sugar
½   teaspoon kosher salt
¼   cup apple cider vinegar
2   tablespoons pure maple syrup
2   teaspoons Dijon mustard
¼   teaspoon black pepper
⅔   cup olive oil
1   (6-ounce) container baby spinach
1   (5-ounce) container mixed greens
1   cup thinly vertically sliced red onion (about 1 onion)
1   (4-ounce) container crumbled goat cheese
¾   cup dried tart cherries

1 Melt butter in a medium skillet over medium. Add almonds; cook, stirring constantly, until almonds just begin to brown, about 3 minutes. Sprinkle almond mixture with sugar; cook, stirring constantly, until sugar melts and mixture caramelizes, 2 to 3 minutes.

2 Spread almond mixture in a single layer on parchment paper.

Sprinkle evenly with ¼ teaspoon of the salt; cool completely, about 10 minutes.

3 Meanwhile, in a small bowl, whisk together vinegar, maple syrup, mustard, pepper, and remaining ¼ teaspoon salt until blended; gradually whisk in oil until fully incorporated.

4 Place spinach and mixed greens in a large serving bowl or on a serving platter. Top with onion, goat cheese, cherries, and almonds. Drizzle with dressing, and serve immediately.

Spiced Gingerbread Latte

Like a gingerbread man in a cup, this hot treat is a delicious morning pick-me-up or after-dinner or après-ski treat. Double this recipe if you wish.

SERVES 4

HANDS-ON 9 MINUTES

TOTAL 21 MINUTES

2   cups whole milk
¼   cup packed light brown sugar
3   cinnamon sticks
2   (1-inch) slices peeled fresh ginger
1   teaspoon ground nutmeg
8   whole cloves
¾   cup (6 ounces) ginger liqueur
2   teaspoons vanilla extract
2½ cups strong-brewed hot coffee or 1 cup espresso
Crystallized ginger pieces, ground cinnamon, or nutmeg (optional)

1 Combine milk, sugar, cinnamon sticks, ginger, nutmeg, and cloves in a small saucepan over medium. Cook, stirring often, until thoroughly heated, about 5 minutes. Remove from heat, and let stand 10 minutes. Pour mixture through a fine wire-mesh strainer, and discard solids. Whisk in ginger liqueur and vanilla. Whisk until frothy, about 1 minute.

❷ Divide coffee evenly among 4 coffee mugs. Top evenly with hot milk mixture. Garnish with crystallized ginger pieces, ground cinnamon, or nutmeg, if desired.

Note: Ginger liqueur can be found at some liquor stores or online specialty stores. You can also use brandy in place of the ginger liqueur, or for a nonalcoholic version, gingerbread-flavored coffee syrup.

Caramelized Apple Cannoli with Praline Sauce

The praline sauce can be made up to 3 days ahead of time and kept chilled. Warm it in a saucepan over low until heated through. Find cannoli shells in the bakery aisle of most supermarkets.

SERVES 10
HANDS-ON 40 MINUTES
TOTAL 1 HOUR, 50 MINUTES

½   **cup (4 ounces) plus 1 tablespoon salted butter**
2   **tablespoons granulated sugar**
1   **tablespoon fresh lemon juice**
2   **large Granny Smith apples, chopped (about 2¾ cups)**
1   **cup packed light brown sugar**
½   **cup half-and-half**
½   **teaspoon vanilla extract**
½   **cup chopped toasted pecans**
1   **(8-ounce) container mascarpone cheese, softened**
½   **cup heavy cream**
1   **tablespoon powdered sugar**
10 **(5-inch-long, ¾-ounce) cannoli shells**

❶ Melt 1 tablespoon of the butter in a large skillet over medium. Add granulated sugar and lemon juice; cook, stirring constantly, until mixture turns a light golden brown, 2 to 3 minutes. Add apples and cook, stirring occasionally, until apples are tender and browned, about 10 minutes. Remove from heat; cool completely, about 20 minutes.

❷ Bring brown sugar, half-and-half, and remaining ½ cup butter to a boil in a medium saucepan over medium, stirring constantly. Cook, stirring constantly, 1 minute. Remove from heat, and stir in vanilla; cool slightly, about 10 minutes. Stir in pecans.

❸ Stir together cooled apple mixture and mascarpone cheese. In a separate bowl, beat cream and powdered sugar with an electric mixer on high speed until soft peaks form, 1 to 2 minutes. Fold whipped cream mixture into apple mixture. (Don't overmix or mixture will curdle.)

❹ Spoon apple-cream mixture into a large ziplock plastic freezer bag; snip 1 corner of bag to make a 1-inch hole. Pipe apple mixture into cannoli shells. Place filled cannoli in a 13- x 9-inch pan. Cover and chill at least 1 hour before serving. Serve cannoli with warm praline sauce.

CHRISTMAS
by the sea

Along the Atlantic and Gulf coasts, Southerners celebrate the season in festive seaside style. Seafood served with a host of red and green trimmings is an elegant feast from start to finish.

THE MENU
serves 6 to 8

SPIKED SATSU-MOSA

SPARKLING BERRIES AND
CHERRIES PUNCH

SMOKED SALMON WITH
FENNEL, CAPERS, AND
LEMON CREAM CHEESE

GRILLED OYSTERS WITH
SMOKY SHERRY BUTTER

ROASTED BRUSSELS
SPROUTS AND RADISHES
WITH LEMON VINAIGRETTE

ROSEMARY-PINK
PEPPERCORN FRENCH LOAF

FINGERLING POTATOES WITH
PICHOLINE OLIVES AND
SHALLOTS

CAESAR WEDGE SALADS
WITH ROASTED RED ONIONS
AND TOMATOES

KEY LIME CHEESECAKE
WITH POMEGRANATE SYRUP

NAUTICAL & NICE

A sandy nod to the season is left on the beach before the tide rolls in. A beach cruiser stands in as a beachside sleigh for delivering gifts.

BELLS & COCKLESHELLS

A palette of aqua and coral with hits of frosty white and the warm sheen of gilded elements usher in the seaside vibe while shells, starfish, and life preserver wreath drive it home.

MAKE WAVES

Garlands of shells swag a mantel accessorized with resin coral that only looks real, while votive holders of turquoise glass dipped in gold and raw linen stockings stamped with sea creatures and personalized with names set the tidal tone. Gift wrap provides another opportunity to accessorize beneath the tree. Bows, barnacles, and ornaments top gifts and hang from flocked boughs, too. Wooden tassel ornaments could fit into any decorating theme, but their sun-bleached finish, reminiscent of driftwood, is perfect here. A bar cart in antique gold does double duty as an appetizer station and is outfitted with all the host or guest needs for a refill.

Spiked Satsu-Mosa; Sparkling Berries and Cherries Punch; Smoked Salmon with Fennel, Capers, and Lemon Cream Cheese

ISLAND FLOURISHES

Shell-covered spheres, buoys, and faux coral add whimsy to a sideboard topped with a lush tropical arrangement.

Clockwise from above: Grilled Oysters with Smoky Sherry Butter, Rosemary-Pink Peppercorn French Loaf, Caesar Wedge Salads with Roasted Red Onions and Tomatoes, Fingerling Potatoes with Picholine Olives and Shallots, Roasted Brussels Sprouts and Radishes with Lemon Vinaigrette

Key Lime Cheesecake
with Pomegranate Syrup

Spiked Satsu-Mosa

Satsumas begin to come into season at the end of November, just in time for the holidays. You can find them at most specialty grocers.

SERVES 6
HANDS-ON 5 MINUTES
TOTAL 5 MINUTES

½ cup fresh satsuma orange juice (1 large or 2 satsumas)
½ cup (4 ounces) citrus-flavored vodka (such as Skyy vodka)
¼ cup ice cubes
3½ cups (28 ounces) Champagne or sparkling wine, chilled

Strain juice through a fine wire-mesh strainer into a cocktail shaker; add vodka and ice cubes. Cover with lid, and shake vigorously until thoroughly chilled, about 30 seconds. Strain about ¼ cup (2 ounces) into each of 6 chilled Champagne flutes. Top evenly with Champagne or sparkling wine.

Sparkling Berries and Cherries Punch

Red fruit juices and bubbly ginger ale make a perfect mocktail.

SERVES 8
HANDS-ON 5 MINUTES
TOTAL 4 HOURS, 5 MINUTES

1½ cups fresh raspberries
¼ cup water
4¾ cups ginger ale
2 cups tart cherry juice, chilled
1 cup lemonade, chilled
Garnishes: lemon slices, fresh raspberries, pitted fresh cherries

❶ Place 2 to 3 raspberries in each compartment of 1 ice-cube tray. Stir together water and ¾ cup of the ginger ale; pour over raspberries. Freeze mixture until firm, about 4 hours.

❷ Combine cherry juice and lemonade in a glass pitcher. Stir in remaining 4 cups ginger ale just before serving. Place ice cubes in 8 glasses; pour punch over ice cubes. Garnish, if desired.

Smoked Salmon with Fennel, Capers, and Lemon Cream Cheese

Capers, lemon, and fennel's sweetness cut through the richness of salmon in this elegant appetizer.

SERVES 6
HANDS-ON 15 MINUTES
TOTAL 30 MINUTES

1 (8.5-ounce) baguette, cut into ½-inch slices
6 tablespoons extra-virgin olive oil
½ teaspoon kosher salt
1 (8-ounce) package cream cheese, softened
2 teaspoons grated lemon zest, plus 2 tablespoons fresh juice (1 large lemon)
1 large fennel bulb, thinly sliced
⅓ cup drained capers
¼ teaspoon black pepper
1 pound thinly sliced smoked salmon
2 tablespoons sliced scallions (optional)

THE SATSUMA

This oh-so-Southern type of mandarin, grown in coastal Louisiana and Alabama, is seedless, easy to peel, and delicately sweet with just the right amount of pucker. The season for this fruit disappears faster than Santa's sleigh, so eat your fill in December. While you're at it, fill a basket or box with this regional gem to give as a gift. It's one the recipient will anticipate year after year.

① Preheat oven to 350°F. Place bread slices in a single layer on a baking sheet; brush with 4 tablespoons of the oil, and sprinkle with ¼ teaspoon of the salt.

② Bake in preheated oven until browned and crisp, 5 to 10 minutes. Remove from oven; set aside.

③ Beat cream cheese and lemon zest with an electric mixer until smooth.

④ Combine fennel, capers, lemon juice, pepper, and remaining ¼ teaspoon salt in a medium bowl, tossing to coat. Chill 15 minutes.

⑤ Arrange smoked salmon slices in a single layer on a chilled serving platter. Spoon fennel mixture over salmon. Drizzle with remaining 2 tablespoons oil. Spread baguette slices with lemon-cream cheese mixture, and serve with salmon and fennel mixture. Sprinkle with scallions, if desired.

Grilled Oysters with Smoky Sherry Butter

Grilling the oysters brings out their sweet, briny flavor which is accented by the smoky compound butter the oysters are topped with. If you'd rather not grill, roast the oysters on a baking sheet at 450°F until the butter is melted and drips over the shell, about 7 minutes.

SERVES 8
HANDS-ON 15 MINUTES
TOTAL 15 MINUTES

1   cup sherry vinegar
2   cups (16 ounces) unsalted butter, softened

¼   cup chopped fresh flat-leaf parsley
2   garlic cloves
1   shallot, chopped
1   tablespoon Worcestershire sauce
2   teaspoons chopped fresh chives
1   teaspoon smoked paprika
½   teaspoon smoked sea salt
¼   teaspoon cayenne pepper
4   dozen large fresh oysters on the half shell
Lemon wedges, fresh flat-leaf parsley (optional)

① Preheat grill to medium-high (about 450°F).

② Bring vinegar to a boil in a small saucepan over medium-high, stirring occasionally. Reduce heat to medium-low, and simmer until syrupy and reduced to about ⅓ cup, about 10 minutes. Cool slightly.

③ Pulse sherry vinegar syrup, butter, parsley, garlic, shallot, Worcestershire, chives, paprika, sea salt, and cayenne in a food processor until well combined.

④ Arrange oysters in a single layer on grill grate; spoon 1 teaspoon butter mixture over each oyster. Grill oysters, uncovered, just until edges curl, about 7 minutes. Serve with lemon wedges, and garnish, if desired.

HOLIDAY HELPER

To shuck an oyster: Hold the oyster in your palm with an oven mitt to prevent cutting yourself, positioning the oyster so that the curved side of the shell faces down and the flat side faces up. Insert a paring or oyster knife between the shells, near the hinge. Twist the knife to detach the muscle. Remove the top shell and use the knife to take the oyster meat out of the bottom shell.

Roasted Brussels Sprouts and Radishes with Lemon Vinaigrette

Heat the grill for this recipe and use it again to grill your oysters. If using the oven, roast at 450°F until tender, about 15 minutes.

SERVES 6
HANDS-ON 20 MINUTES
TOTAL 40 MINUTES

5 to 6 tablespoons olive oil
1½   pounds Brussels sprouts, trimmed and halved
1   pound radishes, trimmed and halved
½   teaspoon lemon zest plus 2 tablespoons fresh juice (from 1 large lemon)
½   teaspoon Dijon mustard
½   teaspoon granulated sugar
¼   teaspoon kosher salt
¼   teaspoon black pepper

① Preheat grill to medium-high (about 450°F). Place an ovenproof or cast-iron skillet on grill.

② Heat 1 tablespoon of the oil in skillet. Add half each of Brussels sprouts and radishes to skillet, and spread in a single layer. Grill, covered, until slightly charred and tender, 8 to 10 minutes, stirring after 4 minutes. Remove vegetables from skillet, and keep warm. Repeat process with remaining Brussels sprouts and radishes, adding 1 tablespoon oil to skillet, if needed.

③ Whisk together lemon zest, lemon juice, mustard, sugar, salt, pepper, and remaining 4 tablespoons oil. Drizzle over vegetables, tossing to coat.

Rosemary-Pink Peppercorn French Loaf

Red and green seasonings add a festive note to this indulgent buttery garlic bread.

SERVES 8

HANDS-ON 5 MINUTES

TOTAL 20 MINUTES

½ cup (4 ounces) salted butter, softened
2 garlic cloves, minced
2 teaspoons chopped fresh rosemary
1 teaspoon pink peppercorns, crushed
1 (12-ounce) French bread loaf

❶ Preheat oven to 375°F. Line a baking sheet with aluminum foil.

❷ Stir together butter, garlic, rosemary, and peppercorns.

❸ Slice bread loaf crosswise at 1-inch intervals, cutting to within ½ inch of the bottom. Spread butter mixture on cut sides and on top of bread, and place on prepared baking sheet.

❹ Bake in preheated oven until butter is melted and bread is crisp and beginning to brown, 10 to 15 minutes.

FRESH IDEA
Swap the fingerling potatoes for parsnips or carrots, cut into chunks, and roast with olives and shallots as directed in the recipe.

Fingerling Potatoes with Picholine Olives and Shallots

Picholine olives are small, green olives that are brine-cured and are often used in cocktails. They can be found in specialty grocers. If Picholine olives are hard to find in stores, you can substitute with plain green or Manzanilla olives (without pimientos).

SERVES 8

HANDS-ON 15 MINUTES

TOTAL 40 MINUTES

2 pounds multicolored fingerling potatoes, cut in half lengthwise
1 cup pitted Picholine olives (or other briny olives)
4 small shallots, peeled and quartered
2 to 3 tablespoons olive oil
2 teaspoons chopped fresh rosemary
½ teaspoon kosher salt
¼ teaspoon black pepper
¼ cup loosely packed fresh flat-leaf parsley leaves (optional)

❶ Preheat oven to 425°F.

❷ Combine potatoes, olives, and shallots in a large bowl. Drizzle with olive oil, tossing to coat. Spread in a single layer on a rimmed baking sheet coated with cooking spray. Sprinkle with rosemary, salt, and pepper.

❸ Bake in preheated oven until potatoes and shallots are browned and tender, 25 to 30 minutes. Sprinkle with parsley leaves, if desired, and serve.

Caesar Wedge Salads with Roasted Red Onions and Tomatoes

Wedge salads are pretty on the plate and, even dressed, hold up well on sideboard buffets.

SERVES 6

HANDS-ON 10 MINUTES

TOTAL 45 MINUTES

8 (¾-inch-thick) French bread slices, cubed
½ cup (4 ounces) salted butter, melted
1 tablespoon chopped fresh flat-leaf parsley
1 tablespoon minced fresh garlic
¾ teaspoon kosher salt
2 medium-size red onions, peeled and cut into ½-inch-thick slices
3 cups grape tomatoes
2 tablespoons olive oil
½ teaspoon black pepper
3 romaine lettuce hearts, cut in half lengthwise
½ cup mayonnaise
2 tablespoons freshly grated Parmigiano-Reggiano cheese
1 tablespoon anchovy paste
1 tablespoon fresh lemon juice
1 tablespoon water
1 teaspoon Dijon mustard

❶ Preheat oven to 350°F. Place bread cubes in a large bowl. Stir together butter, parsley, 1 teaspoon of the garlic, and ¼ teaspoon of the salt. Drizzle butter mixture over bread cubes, tossing to coat. Spread bread cubes in a single layer on a lightly greased aluminum foil-lined rimmed baking sheet.

2 Bake in preheated oven until browned and crisp, 15 to 20 minutes, stirring occasionally. Remove bread from baking sheet; set aside. Increase oven temperature to 425°F.

3 Place onions and tomatoes in a medium bowl. Drizzle with olive oil, tossing to coat. Spread in a single layer on baking sheet; sprinkle with ¼ teaspoon each of the salt and pepper. Bake at 425°F until tomatoes and onions are tender and tomatoes are about to burst, 15 to 20 minutes. Remove from baking sheet; cool slightly. Place romaine halves on a platter. Top with roasted tomatoes and onions.

4 Whisk together mayonnaise, cheese, anchovy paste, lemon juice, water, mustard, and remaining 2 teaspoons garlic and ¼ teaspoon each salt and pepper until smooth. Drizzle over vegetables; top with croutons just before serving.

TIDINGS WE BRING

Cheerful messages in sand-filled bottles are a hopeful nod to the season and the year ahead. Use this beachy accent on an entry table or mantel. Consider dropping in place cards with a holiday wish written on the reverse side and using the bottles on the table to direct guests to their seats.

Key Lime Cheesecake with Pomegranate Syrup

The subtle green of Southern Key lime and the bold red of pomegranate syrup add holiday cheer to this tropical dessert.

SERVES 8
HANDS-ON 1 HOUR, 26 MINUTES
TOTAL 9 HOURS

2   cups graham cracker crumbs
½   cup (4 ounces) salted butter, melted
2   cups granulated sugar
3   (8-ounce) package cream cheese, softened
3   large eggs
1   (8-ounce) container sour cream
1½ teaspoons Key lime zest plus ½ cup fresh juice (about 12 to 15 Key limes)
3   cups refrigerated pomegranate juice
Garnishes: pomegranate arils, Key lime slices, Key lime zest, sweetened whipped cream

1 Preheat oven to 350°F. Stir together graham cracker crumbs, butter, and ¼ cup of the sugar; firmly press mixture on bottom and 2 inches up sides of a greased 9-inch springform pan.

2 Bake in preheated oven 11 minutes; cool on a wire rack, 15 minutes. Reduce oven temperature to 325°F.

3 Beat cream cheese with an electric mixer on medium speed until fluffy; gradually add 1¼ cups of the sugar, beating until blended. Add eggs, 1 at a time, beating well after each addition. Stir in sour cream, lime zest, and juice. Pour batter into crust.

4 Bake at 325°F for 1 hour and 10 minutes; turn oven off. Partially open oven door; let cheesecake stand in oven 15 minutes. Remove from oven, and immediately run a knife around edge of pan, releasing sides of cheesecake.

5 Cool completely in pan on a wire rack, about 2 hours; cover and chill 4 to 8 hours or overnight. Remove sides of pan.

6 Combine pomegranate juice and remaining ½ cup sugar in a medium saucepan over medium-high, stirring until sugar dissolves; bring to a boil. Cook until syrupy and reduced to about 1 cup, about 26 minutes. Cool to room temperature, about 30 minutes. Garnish cheesecake, if desired, and serve with pomegranate syrup.

CHRISTMAS
on the block

Christmas caroling gets everyone in the holiday spirit, but so does a meal shared with neighbors and friends. Fortify a crowd with these hearty, comforting dishes and portable nibbles.

THE MENU
serves 10 to 12

ANTIPASTI SALAD

MUSHROOM-AND-KALE
HAND PIES

OVEN-ROASTED BEEF
TENDERLOIN SLIDERS WITH
HORSERADISH CREAM

SLOW COOKER CHILE VERDE
PULLED PORK TACOS

BAKED PUMPKIN
AND PORCINI RISOTTO

BACON AND CHEDDAR
STUFFED POTATO BITES

HOT BUTTERED RUM

PRALINE HOT CHOCOLATE

LEMON-ALMOND CAKE

TURTLE SHEET CAKE

SET THE SCENE

From driveway to front door, decorations draw guests into this block party and set the tone for a night of caroling, mingling, and fun.

FIRESIDE CHATS

*A cul-de-sac is a perfect landing spot for merry decorations.
A circle of Adirondack chairs around a firepit becomes the
gathering spot to warm up with hot cocoa and conversation.*

RED & GREEN ON EVERYTHING

Traditional holiday colors say "Christmas" at every turn: In the plaid ribbons that tie gift bags holding forced narcissus bulbs for parting favors...in the napkins tucked into pouches for flatware on a serving station...and in woven wool blankets for guests to wrap themselves in as they carol door to door. A small tiered cart on casters is easily rolled to the curb so guests can help themselves to hot cocoa and all the garnishes. A handmade street sign guides drivers and Santa Claus.

Praline Hot Chocolate

Left to right: Slow Cooker Chile Verde Pulled Pork Tacos, Oven-Roasted Beef Tenderloin Sliders with Horseradish Cream, Mushroom-and-Kale Hand Pies, Baked Pumpkin and Porcini Risotto, Antipasti Salad, Bacon and Cheddar Stuffed Potato Bites

Lemon-Almond Cake,
Turtle Sheet Cake

Antipasti Salad

This hearty salad is the best of an antipasti platter all tossed together in a bowl. It tastes even better the day after you make it when the flavors have had a chance to develop. Add or subtract ingredients to suit your taste. Toss in artichoke hearts, use feta in place of the mozzarella, substitute a different fresh herb.

SERVES 14

HANDS-ON 24 MINUTES

TOTAL 1 HOUR, 24 MINUTES

1½ pounds uncooked gemelli pasta (or other short curly pasta)

1 pound fresh small mozzarella cheese balls, drained

6 ounces salami, thinly sliced and quartered

1 cup thinly vertically sliced red onion (from 1 onion)

1 cup torn fresh flat-leaf parsley

½ cup sliced jarred roasted red bell peppers

½ cup sliced green olives

½ cup sliced kalamata olives

⅔ cup red wine vinegar

⅔ cup extra-virgin olive oil

4 teaspoons Dijon mustard

2 teaspoons table salt

1 teaspoon granulated sugar

1 teaspoon black pepper

❶ Cook pasta according to package directions. Drain and rinse with cold water.

❷ Place pasta, mozzarella, salami, onion, parsley, bell peppers, green olives, and kalamata olives in a large bowl; toss to combine.

❸ Whisk together vinegar, oil, mustard, salt, sugar, and black pepper in a small bowl. Drizzle vinaigrette over pasta mixture; toss well to coat. Chill 1 hour before serving.

Note: Make this easy salad the day before serving for better flavor.

Oven-Roasted Beef Tenderloin Sliders with Horseradish Cream

The neighbors will be clamoring to get their mittened hands on these tiny but tasty mini burgers. The lemon zest in the marinade adds a bright citrusy flavor to the beef that works so well with rosemary.

SERVES 12

HANDS-ON 17 MINUTES

TOTAL 2 HOURS, 47 MINUTES

1 (2½-pound) beef tenderloin, trimmed

2 tablespoons olive oil

1 tablespoon chopped fresh rosemary

2 teaspoons lemon zest

1½ teaspoons table salt

1 teaspoon black pepper

1 cup mayonnaise

½ cup sour cream

2 tablespoons prepared horseradish

2 tablespoons chopped fresh chives

1 teaspoon apple cider vinegar

½ teaspoon granulated sugar

24 slider buns, split and toasted

2 cups firmly packed baby arugula

❶ Place beef, oil, rosemary, zest, 1 teaspoon of the salt, and ½ teaspoon of the pepper in a large ziplock plastic freezer bag; seal bag, and massage beef until well coated. Chill 1 hour or up to 8 hours.

❷ Whisk together mayonnaise, sour cream, horseradish, chives, vinegar, sugar, and remaining ½ teaspoon salt and ½ teaspoon pepper in a bowl. Chill until ready to serve.

❸ Remove beef from marinade; discard marinade. Place beef on a rimmed baking sheet coated with cooking spray, and let stand at room temperature 1 hour.

❹ Preheat oven to 425°F. Bake beef until a meat thermometer inserted in thickest portion reads 135°F to 140°F, about 20 minutes.

❺ Remove from oven; let stand 10 minutes. Thinly slice tenderloin, and serve on slider buns with horseradish cream and arugula.

HOLIDAY HELPER

A block party should be a collective effort. Pass out these recipes to those who are able to attend so everyone contributes.

Mushroom-and-Kale Hand Pies

A great pick-up appetizer for any party, savory pies make an impression. If you can't find Lacinato, or dinosaur kale, any variety will do.

SERVES 16 TO 18

HANDS-ON 1 HOUR

TOTAL 2 HOURS, 20 MINUTES

DOUGH

2½ cups (about 10 ¾ ounces) all-purpose flour

4 ounces Parmesan cheese, grated (about 1 cup)

½ teaspoon table salt

¾ cup (6 ounces) cold salted butter, diced

¼ cup vegetable shortening

½ cup ice water

FILLING

1 tablespoon olive oil

1 tablespoon salted butter

8 ounces cremini mushrooms, finely chopped

¼ cup minced shallot

1 teaspoon chopped fresh thyme

1 garlic clove, minced

1 bunch Lacinato kale, stems removed, coarsely chopped (about 4 cups)

½ teaspoon table salt

½ teaspoon black pepper

ADDITIONAL INGREDIENTS

1 large egg

1 teaspoon water

❶ Prepare the Dough: Pulse flour, Parmesan, and salt in a food processor until combined, 3 to 4 times. Add butter and shortening to bowl; pulse until mixture resembles coarse meal, 2 or 3 times. Sprinkle ice water over mixture; pulse until mixture begins to clump together, 2 or 3 times. Scrape dough onto a work surface; knead until dough comes together, 3 or 4 times. Divide dough in half; shape each half into a 4-inch disk. Wrap each dough disk with plastic wrap, and chill at least 1 hour.

❷ Prepare the Filling: Heat oil and butter in a large skillet over medium-high until butter melts. Add mushrooms, shallot, thyme, and garlic; cook, stirring often, until liquid evaporates and mushrooms brown, about 35 minutes. Add kale; cook, stirring occasionally, until kale wilts, about 5 minutes. Stir in salt and pepper. Cool mixture completely.

❸ Prepare the Hand Pies: Preheat oven to 350°F. Remove and discard plastic wrap from 1 dough disk. Roll dough disk into a 16- to 18-inch round. Cut 16 to 18 (⅛-inch-thick) rounds from dough, rerolling scraps 1 time. Place rounds on a parchment paper-lined baking sheet; chill until ready to fill. Remove and discard plastic wrap from second dough disk. Roll dough disk into a 14-inch round. Cut 16 to 18 (⅛-inch-thick) rounds from dough, rerolling scraps 1 time.

❹ Whisk together egg and 1 teaspoon water in a small bowl. Place about 1 to 1½ tablespoons filling in centers of half of the dough rounds. Brush edges of dough with egg mixture. Place remaining dough rounds on top of filling; seal edges with a fork. Brush tops with egg mixture. Using the tip of a knife, make a small slit in the top of each pie for steam to escape.

❺ Bake on parchment-lined baking sheets until browned and crisp, 20 to 30 minutes. Serve warm or at room temperature.

TIME-SAVER

Make the dough and the filling up to two days in advance of the party. Wrap the dough tightly in plastic wrap and cover the filling before refrigerating. When ready to prepare, simply roll and move ahead with Step 3 of recipe.

PASTRY 101

TOUGH: Too little fat, too much water, overmixed, too much flour, or overkneaded

CRUMBLY: Too little water, too much fat, insufficient mixing, or used self-rising flour

SOGGY: Filling too moist, oven temperature too low, or too much liquid in pastry

SHRINKS: Overstretched dough or rolled out to uneven thickness

Slow Cooker Chile Verde Pulled Pork Tacos

This is an easy, flavorful, hands-off braise of pork and chiles that is equally delicious eaten from a bowl with toppings.

SERVES 12

HANDS-ON 37 MINUTES

TOTAL 8 HOURS, 48 MINUTES

4	large poblano peppers
26	corn tortillas
2	cups chopped white onion (from 2 large onions)
6	large tomatillos (about 10 ounces), husked and quartered
5	garlic cloves
2	teaspoons ground cumin
4½	pounds boneless pork shoulder, trimmed
1	teaspoon table salt
1	teaspoon black pepper
1	(10-ounce) package finely shredded cabbage
1½	cups sour cream

❶ Preheat broiler to high with oven rack 6 inches from heat. Place poblanos on an aluminum foil-lined baking sheet; broil until blackened, about 10 minutes, turning occasionally. Wrap poblanos tightly in foil; let stand 10 minutes. Peel poblanos; cut poblanos in half lengthwise, and remove and discard seeds and membranes.

❷ Place 2 tortillas on oven rack 6 inches from heat. Broil until beginning to char, 30 seconds to 1 minute per side. Tear charred tortillas into pieces.

❸ Process poblanos, charred tortillas, onions, tomatillos, garlic, and cumin in a blender or food processor until smooth, about 1 minute.

❹ Sprinkle pork with salt and black pepper. Place in a 5- or 6-quart slow cooker coated with cooking spray. Pour poblano mixture over pork. Cook on LOW until pork is done, about 8 hours.

❺ Skim fat from top of slow cooker, and discard. Remove pork; shred with 2 forks. Place shredded pork in a bowl. Add 1 cup of the poblano mixture from slow cooker to shredded pork; toss to combine. Discard remaining poblano mixture. Warm remaining 24 tortillas according to package directions. Serve pork mixture with warmed tortillas, shredded cabbage, and sour cream.

Baked Pumpkin and Porcini Risotto

Finally, a hands-off risotto! You can buy prechopped butternut squash for even easier prep.

SERVES 12

HANDS-ON 55 MINUTES

TOTAL 1 HOUR, 30 MINUTES

2	cups hot water
1½	ounces dried porcini mushrooms
3	tablespoons olive oil
1	cup chopped shallots (about 5 shallots)
2	tablespoons minced garlic
1	tablespoon chopped fresh thyme
2¼	cups uncooked Arborio rice
¾	cup dry white wine
1	sugar pumpkin (about 1½ pounds), peeled and diced (about 3 cups)
3½	cups chicken stock
2	teaspoons table salt
1	teaspoon black pepper
½	cup heavy cream
4	ounces Parmigiano-Reggiano cheese, grated (about 1 cup)

Thyme sprigs

❶ Place hot water and mushrooms in a bowl; let stand 30 minutes. Drain mushrooms over a bowl, reserving liquid. Finely chop mushrooms.

❷ Preheat oven to 400°F. Heat oil in a Dutch oven over medium-high. Add shallots, garlic, and thyme; cook, stirring constantly, just until beginning to brown, about 6 minutes. Add rice; cook, stirring constantly, until beginning to brown, 4 to 5 minutes. Add wine; cook until liquid almost evaporates, about 1 minute. Add chopped mushrooms and reserved mushroom soaking liquid, pumpkin, stock, salt, and pepper; bring to a boil. Cover Dutch oven, and bake in preheated oven until liquid is absorbed and rice and pumpkin are tender, about 20 minutes.

❸ Stir in cream and ½ cup of the Parmigiano-Reggiano. Top with remaining ½ cup Parmigiano-Reggiano. Sprinkle with thyme sprigs.

Bacon and Cheddar Stuffed Potato Bites

These look and taste like mini twice-baked potatoes and they're perfectly sized for popping into hungry mouths. Look for small new potatoes in uniform sizes, since they often can be quite large. You want to have just ¼-inch rim around the edge of the potato after scooping. Place filling in a ziplock bag and snip off the corner for a disposable piping bag that lets you control the perfect amount of filling.

SERVES 12

HANDS-ON 42 MINUTES

TOTAL 1 HOUR, 17 MINUTES

24 small red new potatoes, halved
2   tablespoons olive oil
1½ teaspoons table salt
½   teaspoon black pepper
1   cup sour cream
4   ounces cream cheese, softened
½   pound bacon, cooked and crumbled
4   ounces sharp Cheddar cheese, grated (about 1 cup)
⅓   cup chopped fresh chives

❶ Preheat oven to 450°F. Place potatoes, oil, 1 teaspoon of the salt, and ¼ teaspoon of the pepper in a large bowl; toss to coat. Arrange potatoes, cut side up, in a single layer on a rimmed baking sheet. Bake until tender, 30 to 35 minutes. Cool slightly.

❷ Using a ½-inch ice-cream scoop or melon baller, scoop 1 to 2 teaspoons potato flesh from center of each potato half, leaving a ¼-inch rim;

place potato flesh in a large bowl. Add sour cream, cream cheese, and remaining ½ teaspoon salt and ¼ teaspoon pepper to bowl; mash with a potato masher to combine. Stir in bacon and Cheddar. Reserve 2 tablespoons chives for garnish; stir remaining chives into potato mixture.

❸ Spoon or pipe mixture evenly into potato shells. Bake in preheated oven until heated through, about 5 minutes. Sprinkle with reserved chives. Serve warm or at room temperature.

Hot Buttered Rum

Keep butter mixture chilled in an airtight container up to 2 weeks.

SERVES 12

HANDS-ON 12 MINUTES

TOTAL 12 MINUTES

1½ cups packed light brown sugar
1   cup (8 ounces) salted butter, softened
½   teaspoon ground cinnamon
½   teaspoon vanilla extract
¼   teaspoon grated fresh nutmeg
6 to 9 cups hot water
3   cups (24 ounces) gold rum

❶ Beat sugar, butter, cinnamon, vanilla, and nutmeg with an electric mixer on medium speed until well combined.

❷ Place 2 tablespoons sugar mixture in each of 12 coffee mugs. Top each with ½ to ¾ cup hot water and ¼ cup rum. Stir well to combine.

Praline Hot Chocolate

Prepare this yummy hot chocolate on the stove, and then place it in a slow cooker on low so it stays warm outdoors and guests can ladle it into mugs themselves. Serve with an assortment of garnishes such as mini marshmallows, peppermints, and cinnamon sticks.

SERVES 12

HANDS-ON 10 MINUTES

TOTAL 40 MINUTES

2   quarts whole milk
1   quart half-and-half
1½ cups packed dark brown sugar
¼   teaspoon table salt
½   vanilla bean, split lengthwise
3   (4-ounce) bittersweet chocolate bars, finely chopped

Combine milk, half-and-half, brown sugar, salt, and vanilla bean in a large Dutch oven over medium-low; bring to a simmer, stirring occasionally. Whisk in chocolate until chocolate melts. Discard vanilla bean before serving.

Lemon-Almond Cake

Use bakery pound cake and jarred lemon curd for an easy, fancy, flavorful layered cake.

SERVES 12
HANDS-ON 20 MINUTES
TOTAL 2 HOURS, 20 MINUTES

½　cup granulated sugar
½　cup water
¼　cup limoncello (lemon liqueur)
2　cups heavy cream
8　ounces cream cheese, softened
½　cup plus 1 tablespoon powdered sugar
1　(10-ounce) jar lemon curd
2　(10-ounce) pound cake loaves, cut into ½-inch-thick slices
1　(4-ounce) white chocolate baking bar, grated (about 1 cup)
1　cup toasted sliced almonds

❶ Bring sugar and water to a boil in a small saucepan over medium. Cook, stirring constantly, until sugar melts, about 1 minute. Pour mixture into a bowl, and stir in limoncello.

❷ Place cream, cream cheese, and ½ cup of the powdered sugar in a bowl; beat with an electric mixer on medium speed until well combined and fluffy. Add curd; beat on low speed until just combined.

❸ Arrange half of pound cake slices in the bottom of a 13- x 9-inch baking dish. Brush pound cake with limoncello mixture. Spread half of whipped cream mixture (about 1½ cups) over top; sprinkle with half of grated chocolate and half of almonds. Repeat process with remaining pound cake slices, limoncello mixture, whipped cream mixture, grated chocolate, and almonds. Sprinkle remaining 1 tablespoon powdered sugar over top. Chill 2 hours before serving.

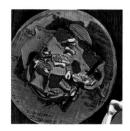

Turtle Sheet Cake

Feed a crowd with this easy yet super-rich sheet cake.

SERVES 12
HANDS-ON 40 MINUTES
TOTAL 1 HOUR, 17 MINUTES

CARAMEL SAUCE
¾　cup packed light brown sugar
¼　cup half-and-half
3　tablespoons salted butter
¼　teaspoon table salt
2　teaspoons vanilla extract

CAKE
2　cups (about 8 ½ ounces) all-purpose flour
1　cup granulated sugar
1　cup packed light brown sugar
⅓　cup unsweetened cocoa
1　teaspoon baking soda
½　teaspoon table salt
¾　cup water
¾　cup (6 ounces) salted butter, melted and cooled
½　cup buttermilk
1　teaspoon vanilla extract
2　large eggs
Baking spray with flour

ICING
½　cup (4 ounces) salted butter
⅓　cup unsweetened cocoa
¼　cup half-and-half
3　cups powdered sugar
½　teaspoon vanilla extract

ADDITIONAL INGREDIENT
½　cup chopped toasted pecans

❶ Prepare the Caramel Sauce: Bring brown sugar, half-and-half, butter, and salt to a boil in a small saucepan over medium-high, stirring often. Cook, stirring often, until mixture thickens slightly, 5 to 6 minutes. Remove from heat. Stir in vanilla; cool completely.

❷ Prepare the Cake: Preheat oven to 375°F. Whisk together flour, sugars, cocoa, baking soda, and salt in a large bowl. Whisk together water, butter, buttermilk, vanilla, and eggs in a separate bowl. Add water mixture to flour mixture; stir just until combined. (Some small lumps may remain.) Spread batter in a 15- x 10-inch jelly-roll pan well coated with baking spray. Bake until a wooden pick inserted in center comes out with moist crumbs, 17 to 20 minutes. Let cool in pan on wire rack.

❸ Prepare the Icing: Bring butter, cocoa, and half-and-half to a boil in a saucepan over medium-high, stirring constantly. Remove from heat. Stir in powdered sugar and vanilla until smooth. Pour icing over warm cake, smoothing to sides of pan. Let stand until icing is cool and firm, about 20 minutes. Drizzle about ½ cup (or more, if desired) Caramel Sauce over cake. Sprinkle with pecans.

HOLIDAY HELPER

A cake mix can be a time-crunched cook's best friend. Don't forget about convenience items like jarred caramel sauce and tubs of frosting. Yes, from-scratch baking is hard to beat, but there is no shame in a sheet cake made from a mix and store-bought embellishments. Guaranteed your guests will dive in and call it "divine!" either way you make it.

Clockwise from above: Pickled Okra Egg Salad
Sandwiches, Cranberry-Tequila Mojito, Cheeseburger
Balls, Sliced Ham and Pickled Onion Skewers

COMPANY'S
coming

We've paired three delicious appetizers—a hot, cold, and quickly-assembled option—with each of three festive craft cocktails so that no matter who's on this year's guest list, you're covered while folks mix and mingle.

Pear-and-Prosecco Cocktail

Clockwise from top: Cranberry-Brie Crostini, Bacon-Cheese Pull-Apart Bread Bites, Feta Cheese and Tomato Tarts

Clockwise from above: Rum Eggnog;
Scallop-and-Bacon Sandwiches;
Pear, Havarti, and Fig Bites; Goat
Cheese with Pistachios and Honey

Cranberry-Tequila Mojito

The mint and lime in this visually stunning drink add a nice fresh note, and cranberry syrup adds a tart-sweet sensation. Swap the tequila for vodka or gin if you like, keeping the other components the same.

SERVES 2

HANDS-ON 5 MINUTES

TOTAL 25 MINUTES

½ cup granulated sugar
⅓ cup water
¾ cup fresh cranberries
½ lime, cut into wedges
8 fresh mint leaves
1 cup seltzer water
½ cup (4 ounces) silver tequila

❶ Combine sugar, water, and ½ cup of the cranberries in a small saucepan; bring to a boil over high, stirring to dissolve sugar. Reduce heat to medium, and cook 5 minutes, stirring occasionally. Remove from heat; let stand 15 minutes. Remove cranberries, and discard.

❷ Divide lime wedges and mint between 2 tall glasses. Muddle together until lime starts to soften. Divide remaining ¼ cup cranberries between glasses. Fill each glass with ice, ½ cup seltzer water, 2 ounces tequila, and half of sugar mixture.

Pear-and-Prosecco Cocktail

This refreshing, effervescent aperitif is perfect for toasting guests and pairs well with cheese and crackers.

SERVES 6

HANDS-ON 15 MINUTES

TOTAL 30 MINUTES

½ cup water
½ cup finely chopped peeled pear
⅓ cup sugar
¼ cup (2 ounces) pear liqueur
6 thin pear slices
1 (750-milliliter) bottle prosecco, chilled

Combine water, chopped pear, and sugar in a small saucepan; bring to a boil over high. Reduce heat to low, and simmer 5 minutes. Remove from heat, and let stand 10 minutes. Pour through a fine wire-mesh strainer into a measuring cup; discard solids. Stir in liqueur. Divide evenly among 6 Champagne flutes. Place 1 pear slice in each glass, and top with prosecco.

Rum Eggnog

Rich and creamy, this new spin on the traditional holiday nog uses rum instead of bourbon. A vigorous shake in a cocktail shaker lends an airy froth to the mix that lightens its usual richness.

SERVES 2

HANDS-ON 5 MINUTES

TOTAL 35 MINUTES

¼ cup 2% reduced-fat milk
½ cup refrigerated eggnog
¼ teaspoon ground cinnamon, plus more for garnish
¼ teaspoon vanilla extract
⅛ teaspoon ground nutmeg, plus more for garnish
6 tablespoons (3 ounces) gold rum

❶ Combine milk, eggnog, cinnamon, vanilla, and nutmeg in a small saucepan; bring to a simmer over medium. Remove from heat; let stand 10 minutes. Chill completely, about 20 minutes.

❷ Combine milk mixture and rum in an ice-filled cocktail shaker; shake vigorously for 30 seconds. Strain into 2 glasses. Garnish with ground cinnamon and nutmeg, if desired.

Sliced Ham and Pickled Onion Skewers

Antipasti on a skewer is fast finger food. Vinegar from the pickled onions balances the richness of the salami. Substitute other types of cured meats or add a mozzarella pearl.

SERVES 4

HANDS-ON 5 MINUTES

TOTAL 5 MINUTES

8   slices salami (about 1 ¾ ounces)
4   slices deli ham (about 2 ounces)
12 pickled onions
4   jarred roasted red bell peppers, each cut into 3 (1-inch) squares
12 pimiento-stuffed olives
12 (4-inch) skewers

Place 2 salami slices on 1 ham slice. Roll up, and cut into 3 wheels. Repeat with remaining ham and salami slices. Thread 1 ham-salami wheel, 1 onion, 1 pepper slice, and 1 olive onto each skewer.

Cheeseburger Balls

Make the meat mixture ahead of time and shape when ready to bake. Serve with wooden picks.

SERVES 10

HANDS-ON 15 MINUTES

TOTAL 30 MINUTES

6   thick-cut bacon slices, finely chopped
1   pound ground chuck
2   ounces Cheddar cheese, shredded (about ½ cup)
2   ounces Parmesan cheese, grated (about ½ cup)
¼   cup chopped fresh flat-leaf parsley
1   tablespoon Worcestershire sauce
1   teaspoon garlic powder
½   teaspoon table salt
½   teaspoon black pepper
10 round buttery crackers (such as Ritz), ground in a food processor
2   large eggs

❶ Cook bacon in a skillet over medium until crisp; remove from heat. Remove bacon from pan with a slotted spoon, and drain on paper towels, reserving 2 tablespoons drippings. Cool bacon and drippings 10 minutes.

❷ Preheat oven to 400°F. Combine ground chuck, Cheddar, Parmesan, parsley, Worcestershire sauce, garlic powder, salt, pepper, crushed crackers, eggs, crumbled bacon, and reserved drippings in a medium bowl, and stir gently to combine. Shape mixture into 30 (1-inch) meatballs. Place about 1 inch apart in a single layer on a large rimmed baking sheet. Bake in preheated oven to desired degree of doneness, about 15 minutes.

Feta Cheese and Tomato Tarts

The tomato mixture for this one-bite appetizer can be made ahead and left to marinate. It's pretty terrific tossed with hot cooked pasta, too!

SERVES 15

HANDS-ON 5 MINUTES

TOTAL 15 MINUTES

2   tablespoons extra-virgin olive oil
2   tablespoons balsamic vinegar
2   teaspoons honey
1   teaspoon minced garlic (1 small garlic clove)
½   teaspoon table salt
½   teaspoon black pepper
1¾ cups coarsely chopped heirloom cherry tomatoes (about 8½ ounces)
¼   cup chopped fresh chives
2   ounces feta cheese, crumbled (about ½ cup)
2   (1.9-ounce) packages fully baked mini phyllo pastry shells (such as Athens Mini Fillo Shells)

Whisk together oil, vinegar, honey, garlic, salt, and pepper in a medium bowl. Add tomatoes and chives; toss to coat. Let stand 10 minutes. Add feta, and toss to coat. Divide tomato mixture evenly among pastry shells.

HOLIDAY HELPER

Stock the pantry with olives, pickles, tapenades, and crackers so you can quickly assemble nibbles for unexpected guests.

Cranberry-Brie Crostini

This pretty and simple-to-make crostini can be assembled and ready for guests in 5 minutes tops. Try this with goat cheese and any other kind of fruit relish or jam.

SERVES 8
HANDS-ON 5 MINUTES
TOTAL 5 MINUTES

16 (½-inch-thick) diagonally sliced French bread slices
4 ounces triple-cream Brie (such as Saint Angel), at room temperature
¼ cup plus 4 teaspoons cranberry relish (such as Stonewall Kitchen)
1 tablespoon honey
1 tablespoon fresh thyme leaves

Preheat broiler with oven rack about 6 inches from heat. Place bread in a single layer on a baking sheet; broil until lightly toasted, 1 to 2 minutes on each side. Spread Brie evenly on 1 side of each bread slice. Top each with about 1 teaspoon relish. Drizzle with honey, and sprinkle with thyme leaves.

Note: For your guests who might like a lower carb option, spread the softened Brie on Granny Smith apple slices and then top with the relish and fresh thyme leaves.

Bacon-Cheese Pull-Apart Bread Bites

A collision of deliciousness in a new, favorite appetizer.

SERVES 12
HANDS-ON 10 MINUTES
TOTAL 30 MINUTES

8 thick-cut bacon slices, chopped
½ cup mayonnaise
1 (0.4-ounce) envelope buttermilk Ranch dressing mix
12 ounces Monterey Jack cheese, shredded (about 3 cups)
1 large loaf soft bread, unsliced
3 tablespoons chopped fresh flat-leaf parsley

❶ Preheat oven to 400°F. Cook bacon in a large skillet over medium-high until crisp, 10 to 15 minutes. Remove bacon from pan with a slotted spoon, and drain on paper towels, reserving 3 tablespoons of drippings. Stir together mayonnaise, Ranch dressing mix, and reserved drippings in a medium bowl. Crumble bacon; add bacon and cheese to mayonnaise mixture, stirring to combine.

❷ Cut 1-inch slices through the top of bread to, but not through, the bottom. Turn bread 90° and cut 1-inch slices to create a crosshatch pattern. Using your fingers, gently expand openings in bread. Place bread on a baking sheet lined with aluminum foil. Press cheese mixture into openings in bread loaf, partially filling gaps. Bake in preheated oven until cheese is completely melted, about 20 minutes. Sprinkle with parsley.

Scallop-and-Bacon Sandwiches

Halved scallops become the "bun" for this fun seaside spin on a BLT slider. The cocktail picks keep it all together for presentation and easy eating. Keep these little bites at ideal temperature by serving on a warm platter.

SERVES 4
HANDS-ON 15 MINUTES
TOTAL 15 MINUTES

4 thick-cut bacon slices
12 large dry-packed sea scallops
½ teaspoon black pepper
¼ teaspoon table salt
3 tablespoons mayonnaise
1 tablespoon coarse-grain mustard
12 baby spinach leaves, stems removed
Sliced plum tomatoes (optional)
12 decorative cocktail picks

❶ Cook bacon in a large cast-iron skillet over medium-high until crisp. Remove bacon from pan, and drain on paper towels, reserving drippings in skillet. Sprinkle scallops with pepper and salt. Increase heat to high. Add scallops to skillet; cook 2 minutes on each side.

❷ Combine mayonnaise and mustard in a small bowl. Slice scallops in half horizontally. Break each bacon slice into 3 pieces. On bottom half of each scallop, place 1 teaspoon mayonnaise mixture, 1 spinach leaf, 1 bacon piece, and, if desired, 1 tomato slice. Cover with top half of scallop. Place a cocktail pick through each sandwich, and serve.

Goat Cheese with Pistachios and Honey

This quick and tasty gussied up goat cheese is a pretty addition to the cocktail table and so easy to prepare. Pistachios add the perfect crunch to this creamy, salty-sweet combo. Substitute toasted pecans or walnuts for a change of pace.

SERVES 12

HANDS-ON 5 MINUTES

TOTAL 5 MINUTES

1   (8-ounce) goat cheese log
2   tablespoons honey
1   tablespoon balsamic glaze (page 23)
¼   cup chopped pistachios
1   teaspoon chopped fresh thyme
¼   teaspoon coarse salt
¼   teaspoon coarsely ground black pepper
24   round buttery crackers (such as Ritz) or 24 baguette slices

Slice goat cheese crosswise into 12 slices. Arrange, slightly overlapping, on shallow plate. Drizzle with honey and balsamic glaze. Sprinkle with pistachios, thyme, salt, and pepper. Serve with crackers or bread slices.

Pickled Okra Egg Salad Sandwiches

Pickled okra stands in for the usual pickle relish in this zesty egg salad. Make the egg salad ahead of time and then spread on toasts just before serving.

SERVES 16

HANDS-ON 20 MINUTES

TOTAL 1 HOUR

6   large eggs
12   white bread slices (about 18 ounces)
¼   cup mayonnaise
¼   cup chopped fresh chives
¼   cup chopped pickled okra
1   tablespoon fresh lemon juice
1   tablespoon pickled okra liquid from jar
2   teaspoons Dijon mustard
¾   teaspoon table salt
¾   teaspoon black pepper
8   pickled okra pods, diagonally sliced (optional)
Shaved radishes, celery leaves, basil leaves, parsley leaves (optional)

❶ Add water to a depth of 1 inch to a medium saucepan fitted with a steamer basket; bring to a boil over high. Add eggs to steamer basket; cover and cook 12 minutes. Plunge eggs into ice water; let stand 15 minutes. Peel eggs, and chop.

❷ Preheat broiler with oven rack about 6 inches from heat. Using a 1½-inch round cutter, cut bread into 64 circles; discard remaining bread. Place bread circles in a single layer on baking sheets; broil until lightly browned, 1 to 2 minutes per side.

❸ Stir together mayonnaise, chives, pickled okra, lemon juice, pickled okra liquid, mustard, salt, and pepper in a medium bowl. Add chopped eggs, and stir gently to combine. Top each piece of toast with about 1 teaspoon egg salad. Garnish, if desired.

Pear, Havarti, and Fig Bites

The dense creamy texture of Havarti paired with sweet, juicy pear and a fig drizzle is a sure-to-be-devoured bet for any gathering. This is an easy appetizer to throw together when the doorbell rings and is a nice alternative to a fruit and cheese platter.

SERVES 12

HANDS-ON 5 MINUTES

TOTAL 5 MINUTES

1   large pear, cut into 24 (½-inch) cubes
12   (½-inch) cubes Havarti cheese
12   decorative cocktail picks
4   tablespoons fig preserves
2   tablespoons lemon juice

Thread 1 pear cube, 1 cheese cube, and another pear cube on each cocktail pick; place on a platter. Stir together fig preserves and lemon juice, and lightly drizzle over pear-cheese cocktail picks.

Chicken Cacciatore with Peppers and Olives

SLOW-COOKED
comforts

Chilly winter nights demand a warm, satisfying meal that doesn't relegate the cook to the kitchen. These delectable main attractions involve mostly hands-off time to simmer, braise, and transform into mealtime perfection.

Sage and Cream Braised Pork Loin,
Bourbon-Orange Glazed Brisket

Veal Osso Buco

Mustard and White Wine
Braised Chicken Thighs

Beer-Braised
Beef Short Ribs

Hearty Beef Stew

Braised Lamb Leg

Sage and Cream Braised Pork Loin

This dish conjures formal dinners at Downton Abbey, but it is admittedly pretty tasty whatever side of the pond you reside.

SERVES 4
HANDS-ON 35 MINUTES
TOTAL 3 HOURS, 35 MINUTES

- 1 (4- to 5-pound) bone-in pork loin roast
- 2 teaspoons kosher salt
- 1 teaspoon freshly ground black pepper
- 1 tablespoon salted butter
- 1 tablespoon olive oil
- ¼ cup chopped fresh sage
- 2 cups whole milk
- 2 cups heavy cream
- 2 (2-inch) lemon peel strips
- 2 teaspoons cornstarch
- 2 teaspoons water
- Fresh sage leaves (optional)

❶ Sprinkle roast with salt and pepper. Melt butter with oil in a large Dutch oven over medium-high; add roast and cook, turning to brown on all sides, about 10 minutes.

❷ Sprinkle sage over roast, and cook 30 seconds. Add milk, cream, and lemon peel strips; bring to a simmer. Cover, reduce heat to low, and cook until roast is tender, about 2 hours and 30 minutes, turning roast twice. Turn roast again, and simmer, uncovered, until roast is very tender, about 30 minutes.

❸ Remove roast from Dutch oven; let stand 10 minutes before slicing. Meanwhile, increase heat to medium-high. Boil sauce until just thickened, about 15 minutes. Whisk together cornstarch and water; gradually add to boiling sauce, and cook, whisking constantly, 1 minute. Remove from heat.

❹ Slice roast evenly into chops; drizzle sauce over pork. Garnish with sage leaves, if desired.

Mustard and White Wine Braised Chicken Thighs

Chicken thighs simmered in wine sauce become sublime and delicious.

SERVES 4
HANDS-ON 45 MINUTES
TOTAL 1 HOUR, 30 MINUTES

- ¼ cup all-purpose flour
- 2 teaspoons kosher salt
- ¾ teaspoon black pepper
- 8 skinless, bone-in chicken thighs
- 3 tablespoons olive oil
- 1 yellow onion, sliced
- 1 large leek, trimmed, halved lengthwise, and sliced
- 3 garlic cloves, minced
- 1 cup dry white wine
- 1 cup chicken stock
- 3 tablespoons stone-ground or grainy mustard
- 6 thyme sprigs
- 1½ teaspoons chopped fresh rosemary
- 1 tablespoon chopped fresh flat-leaf parsley
- Hot cooked rice

❶ Combine flour, 1 teaspoon of the salt, and ½ teaspoon of the pepper in a shallow dish. Dredge chicken thighs, 1 at a time, in flour mixture until well coated; reserve remaining flour mixture in dish.

❷ Heat 1 tablespoon of the oil in a large Dutch oven over medium-high. Add 4 chicken thighs, and cook until browned, about 5 minutes per side. Remove browned chicken thighs to a plate, and repeat procedure with 1 tablespoon oil and remaining 4 uncooked chicken thighs.

❸ Add remaining 1 tablespoon oil to hot drippings in Dutch oven over medium-high. Add onion, leek, and garlic; cook, stirring occasionally, until tender and beginning to brown, about 7 minutes. Sprinkle reserved flour mixture over vegetables, and cook, stirring constantly, 1 minute. Add wine, stirring to loosen brown bits from bottom of Dutch oven. Cook, stirring often, until wine has reduced by half, 3 to 4 minutes. Stir in chicken stock, mustard, thyme sprigs, rosemary, and remaining 1 teaspoon salt and ¼ teaspoon pepper; return to a boil.

❹ Nestle chicken into sauce in Dutch oven. Reduce heat to medium-low; cover and simmer until meat is very tender and pulls away easily from bone, about 45 minutes. Sprinkle with parsley just before serving, and serve over hot cooked rice.

Braised Lamb Leg

An impressive star attraction for any gathering, a whole leg of lamb is a classic on the holiday table. Braising versus roasting yields an entirely different texture to the finished dish.

SERVES 8

HANDS-ON 52 MINUTES

TOTAL 3 HOURS, 14 MINUTES

1   (6-pound) whole lamb leg, trimmed
2   tablespoons olive oil
2¼ teaspoons kosher salt
2   teaspoons black pepper
8   carrots, peeled and sliced
1½ pounds pearl onions, peeled (about 2½ cups)
8   garlic cloves, minced
3   cups dry white wine
3   cups beef stock
2   pounds baby new or red potatoes
4   rosemary sprigs
4   thyme sprigs
3   bay leaves
3   tablespoons cold water
3   tablespoons cornstarch

❶ Preheat oven to 325°F. Rub lamb with 2 teaspoons of the oil, and sprinkle with salt and pepper.

❷ Heat remaining 4 teaspoons oil in a large Dutch oven over medium-high. Add the lamb and brown on all sides, 10 minutes; Remove.

❸ Add carrots and onions to hot pan drippings, and cook, stirring often, until just tender, about 5 minutes. Add garlic, and cook, stirring constantly, 1 minute. Stir in wine, stock, potatoes, rosemary, thyme, and bay leaves; bring mixture to

a boil. Remove from heat. Return lamb to Dutch oven, and cover with a tight-fitting lid.

❹ Bake in preheated oven on lower oven rack until meat is very tender and pulls away from bone, 2 hours and 30 minutes to 3 hours, turning lamb once. Carefully transfer lamb to a serving platter. Using a slotted spoon, transfer vegetables onto platter; keep warm.

❺ Pour cooking liquid through a fine wire-mesh strainer into a saucepan; discard solids. Bring to a boil over medium-high, and boil, stirring occasionally, until sauce reduces slightly, about 10 minutes. Stir together water and cornstarch in a small bowl until a paste forms. Add mixture to cooking liquid, whisking until smooth. Bring to a boil; reduce heat to medium-low, and simmer, stirring constantly, until sauce thickens slightly, 1 to 2 minutes. Serve lamb with sauce.

DID YOU KNOW?

Braising is a moist-heat method of browning and searing meat in fat, then covering and simmering in a small amount of liquid over low heat on the stovetop or in the oven. Braising transforms inexpensive cuts of meat into something fall-off-the-bone tender with minimal effort (think pot roast). Braises are even better when prepared a day in advance, allowing flavors to really come together. When preparing ahead, store the meat in the braising liquid, covered, in the refrigerator to keep it from drying out.

Bourbon-Orange Glazed Brisket

The brisket can be served pulled and sandwiched in a bun.

SERVES 6

HANDS-ON 40 MINUTES

TOTAL 8 HOURS

1   (3-pound) beef brisket
1   tablespoon kosher salt
¾ teaspoon black pepper
2   cups vertically sliced onion (about 1 large)
1   cup beef broth
½ cup bourbon or whiskey
1   tablespoon plus 1 teaspoon balsamic vinegar
5   bay leaves
½ cup orange marmalade

❶ Rub brisket with 2 teaspoons of the salt and ½ teaspoon of the pepper. Coat a large, heavy skillet with cooking spray, and place over medium-high. Add brisket to skillet; cook, browning on all sides, about 10 minutes. Transfer beef to a 6-quart slow cooker. Add onion and remaining 1 teaspoon salt and ¼ teaspoon pepper to skillet; cook until tender, about 5 minutes. Add beef broth, bourbon, and 1 tablespoon of the balsamic vinegar to skillet, stirring to loosen browned bits from bottom. Bring to a boil, and cook 4 minutes. Pour mixture over beef; add bay leaves.

❷ Cover and cook on LOW until tender, but not falling apart, 7 hours to 7 hours and 30 minutes. Discard bay leaves. Cut brisket diagonally across the grain into thin slices.

❸ Pour cooking liquid through a wire-mesh strainer into a medium

FRESH VS. DRIED HERBS

If you want to use dried herbs for fresh in a recipe, it helps to know that you should use considerably less as dried herbs have a more potent, concentrated flavor. Typically, you decrease the amount of fresh herbs called for by about two-thirds. So if your recipe calls for 1½ teaspoons fresh thyme, you would use only ½ teaspoon of dried thyme in its place.

saucepan, discarding solids. Boil over medium-high and then simmer until reduced by half, about 20 minutes. Stir in marmalade and remaining 1 teaspoon balsamic vinegar; simmer until slightly thickened, about 5 minutes. Serve beef with sauce.

Chicken Cacciatore with Peppers and Olives

Cacciatore means "hunter" in Italian. Some renditions have tomatoes and mushrooms in the mix, but here bell peppers and olives shine.

SERVES 4
HANDS-ON 31 MINUTES
TOTAL 2 HOURS, 5 MINUTES

1   (4-pound) whole chicken, cut up
1   teaspoon kosher salt
1   teaspoon freshly ground black pepper
1   cup (about 4¼ ounces) all-purpose flour
2   tablespoons olive oil
2   red bell peppers, cut into ½-inch strips

2   green bell peppers, cut into ½-inch strips
1   large yellow onion, halved and vertically sliced
3   garlic cloves, minced
½   cup pitted kalamata or Niçoise olives, coarsely chopped
1½   cups dry red wine
1   cup chicken stock
¼   cup coarsely chopped fresh flat-leaf parsley
2   tablespoons chopped fresh thyme
1   bay leaf
1   tablespoon cornstarch
1   tablespoon water
Hot cooked linguine

❶ Sprinkle chicken with salt and pepper. Dredge in flour, shaking off excess.

❷ Heat 1 tablespoon of the oil in a large Dutch oven over medium-high. Cook chicken, in batches, until browned, 3 to 5 minutes on each side. Transfer to a plate.

❸ Add remaining 1 tablespoon oil to Dutch oven, and heat over medium. Add bell peppers and onion, and cook, stirring occasionally, until peppers are almost tender, about 5 minutes. Add garlic, and cook 30 seconds. Stir in olives. Return chicken to Dutch oven; add wine, stock, parsley, thyme, and bay leaf.

❹ Bring to a simmer. Cover, reduce heat to medium-low, and cook until chicken is done and meat is tender enough to fall off the bone, about 1 hour and 30 minutes, basting chicken occasionally with liquid in

Dutch oven. Remove chicken. Cook liquid in Dutch oven until reduced to about 2½ cups. Whisk together cornstarch and water; whisk into cooking liquid until thickened, about 5 minutes. Remove and discard bay leaf. Return chicken to Dutch oven. Serve chicken mixture over linguine.

FRESH IDEA

For a change of pace, serve rustic Chicken Cacciatore over a bed of hot cooked polenta—the Italian version of our Southern grits—for a soul-satisfying hearty meal.

Veal Osso Buco

This special occasion braise is delicious over grits or polenta.

SERVES 6
HANDS-ON 45 MINUTES
TOTAL 2 HOURS, 10 MINUTES

¼ cup all-purpose flour
2 teaspoons kosher salt
1½ teaspoons black pepper
6 (1-inch-thick) veal shanks (about 2½ to 3 pounds)
6 tablespoons olive oil
1 large yellow onion, diced (about 2 cups)
2 medium carrots, peeled and diced (about 1 cup)
3 medium celery stalks, diced (about 1 cup)
4 garlic cloves, minced
2 tablespoons tomato paste
2 cups dry red wine
2 cups beef stock
2 teaspoons finely chopped fresh rosemary
2 teaspoons finely chopped fresh thyme
2 teaspoons finely chopped fresh basil
3 tablespoons chopped fresh flat-leaf parsley
1 teaspoon lemon zest

❶ Preheat oven to 350°F. Combine flour, 1 teaspoon of the salt, and ¾ teaspoon of the pepper in a ziplock plastic freezer bag. Add 1 shank at a time to bag, shaking to coat with flour mixture. Reserve remaining flour mixture in bag.

❷ Heat 2 tablespoons of the oil in a large ovenproof Dutch oven over medium-high. Add 3 veal shanks, and cook until browned, about 3 minutes per side. Transfer browned shanks to a plate, and repeat procedure with 2 tablespoons oil and remaining 3 uncooked veal shanks. Set veal aside.

❸ Heat remaining 2 tablespoons oil in Dutch oven over medium-high. Add onion, carrots, celery, and garlic; cook, stirring often, until onion is tender, about 8 minutes. Stir in tomato paste; cook 1 minute. Stir in wine, and bring to a boil. Cook, stirring often, until reduced by half, about 8 minutes. Sprinkle vegetable mixture with reserved flour mixture in bag, and cook, stirring constantly, 30 seconds. Add beef stock, rosemary, thyme, basil, and remaining 1 teaspoon salt and ¾ teaspoon pepper, and bring to a boil. Remove from heat.

❹ Nestle veal shanks into vegetable mixture in Dutch oven; cover and bake in preheated oven until veal is tender, about 1 hour and 15 minutes. Remove from oven, and let stand, covered, 10 minutes. Combine parsley and lemon zest; sprinkle over veal.

Hearty Beef Stew

This dish elevates the slow cooker to an all-star appliance and the cook to top chef.

SERVES 8
HANDS-ON 30 MINUTES
TOTAL 7 HOURS

⅓ cup (about 1½ ounces) all-purpose flour
½ teaspoon garlic powder
1 tablespoon plus 2 teaspoons kosher salt
1 teaspoon black pepper
2½ pounds chuck roast, cut into 1-inch cubes
2 tablespoons vegetable oil
2 medium-size yellow onions, halved and sliced (about 3 cups)
1 cup dry red wine
1 cup beef broth
2 garlic cloves, minced
1 pound carrots, peeled and cut into 1-inch pieces (about 2 cups)
1 pound small golden or red potatoes, quartered (about 4 cups)
3 tablespoons tomato paste
8 thyme sprigs
4 bay leaves
2 (15-ounce) cans Great Northern or other white beans, drained

VEAL 101

Veal is beef from young calves with a mild flavor and buttery texture. The best quality veal is very pale pink in color. It requires careful cooking because its lack of fat can cause it to become tough and dry. Veal roasts and shanks respond best to long, slow braising. Prime veal, the highest quality, has been milk-fed. Choice veal has been grain-fed.

➊ Combine flour, garlic powder, 2 teaspoons of the salt, and ½ teaspoon of the pepper in a ziplock plastic bag. Add beef to bag; seal bag, shaking to coat beef. Heat 1 tablespoon of the oil in a large skillet over medium-high. Add half of beef, and cook, turning until browned on all sides. Remove beef from skillet. Repeat with remaining oil and beef; transfer all beef to a 6-quart slow cooker.

➋ Add onions, 1 teaspoon salt, and remaining ½ teaspoon pepper to skillet; cook until tender, about 5 minutes. Add wine, stirring to loosen browned bits from bottom of skillet; stir in beef broth. Pour mixture over beef in slow cooker.

➌ Add garlic, carrots, potatoes, tomato paste, thyme, and bay leaves to slow cooker. Cover and cook on LOW until beef is tender, 6 hours to 6 hours and 30 minutes. Discard bay leaves and thyme sprigs. Stir in beans and remaining 2 teaspoons salt; cook until beans are heated through, about 30 minutes.

FRESH IDEA

Leftover beef stew is delicious served sloppy Joe style on buns and topped with Cheddar cheese for another comforting meal.

Beer-Braised Beef Short Ribs

The black peppercorns and brown sugar offset the bitterness of the stout beer in this rich, savory beef dish. If a stout beer is not to your liking, try a darker lager instead.

SERVES 4
HANDS-ON 29 MINUTES
TOTAL 4 HOURS, 9 MINUTES

2   teaspoons kosher salt
2   teaspoons cracked black peppercorns
3½ to 4 pounds beef short ribs, trimmed (about 6 to 8 ribs)
2   tablespoons olive oil
1   large yellow onion, chopped (about 3 cups)
5   garlic cloves, minced
2   tablespoons tomato paste
1   tablespoon brown sugar
2   (12-ounce) bottles stout beer
2   cups beef stock
1½ pounds carrots, peeled and cut diagonally into 2-inch pieces
3   thyme sprigs
1   bay leaf

➊ Preheat oven to 300°F. Combine salt and pepper; sprinkle on all sides of ribs.

➋ Heat 1 tablespoon of the oil in a large ovenproof Dutch oven over medium-high. Add half of ribs, and cook until browned, about 3 minutes per side. Remove ribs to a plate. Repeat procedure with remaining oil and ribs.

➌ Add onion to hot drippings in Dutch oven, and cook, stirring often, until tender, about 5 minutes. Add garlic, and cook, stirring constantly,

1 minute. Add tomato paste and brown sugar; cook, stirring often, 1 minute. Stir in beer and beef stock.

➍ Place ribs, meat side down, in liquid in Dutch oven. Add carrots, thyme sprigs, and bay leaf; bring to a simmer over high heat. Place a piece of parchment paper directly on beef mixture, and cover Dutch oven with a tight-fitting lid.

➎ Bake in preheated oven until meat is tender and pulls away from bone, 3 hours to 3 hours and 30 minutes. Remove from oven; let ribs stand in Dutch oven, covered, 30 minutes.

➏ Remove parchment paper. Transfer ribs to a serving platter. Spoon carrots around ribs; cover with foil. Skim fat from cooking liquid, and discard. Pour liquid through a fine wire-mesh strainer into a large saucepan; discard solids. Bring to a simmer over medium-high, and simmer, whisking occasionally, until sauce reduces slightly, about 10 minutes. Remove from heat. Serve sauce with ribs.

DID YOU KNOW?

It is thought that the Dutch oven is of Pennsylvania Dutch heritage. Traditionally, the flat-lidded cast-iron vessel had 3 legs for resting above the coals of a fire and a ridge in the lid for holding coals on top. Similar cooking vessels are called "casseroles" in England, "cocottes" in France, and "braadpan" in the Netherlands.

Wild Rice and Cranberry Salad, Bourbon-Pecan Mashed Sweet Potatoes, Green Beans with Brie Cream Sauce and Fried Shallots

SHOWSTOPPING
sides

No holiday feast is complete without the perfect accompaniment. The side dishes are often the most anticipated favorites on the table. From warm purees and starches to vibrant veggies and crisp salads, we've got it all.

Clockwise from left: Butter-Braised Celery, Broccolini with Pancetta and Breadcrumbs, Mushroom Medley with Butter-Brandy Sauce and Parmesan

Potatoes Anna with Caramelized Onion Gravy

Bourbon-Pecan Mashed Sweet Potatoes

Peeling sweet potatoes is a breeze when you boil them whole; their jackets slip right off when cooled. They may take longer to cook than when peeled and cubed, but it's hands-off time so you can prep other recipes.

SERVES 6 TO 8
HANDS-ON 45 MINUTES
TOTAL 1 HOUR, 45 MINUTES

1   medium egg white
2   tablespoons bourbon
6   tablespoons packed light brown sugar
1   cup pecan halves
1¼ teaspoons kosher salt
2   pounds small sweet potatoes (about 3 potatoes)
¼   cup (2 ounces) salted butter, softened

❶ Preheat oven to 275°F. Whisk egg white in a medium bowl until foamy; whisk in bourbon and 2 tablespoons of the brown sugar. Add pecans, tossing to coat.

❷ Spread pecans in a single layer on a parchment paper-lined baking sheet; sprinkle with ¼ teaspoon of the salt. Bake until toasted, 35 to 40 minutes, stirring occasionally. Remove pecans from pan.

❸ Place sweet potatoes in a large Dutch oven; add water to cover. Cover Dutch oven, and bring water to a boil. Boil, uncovered, until potatoes are very tender, 20 to 25 minutes; drain, and cool to the touch, about 30 minutes. Peel sweet potatoes.

❹ Combine sweet potatoes, butter, and remaining ¼ cup brown sugar and 1 teaspoon salt in a large bowl; mash with a potato masher until smooth. Spoon sweet potato mixture into a serving bowl, and sprinkle with bourbon pecans.

Wild Rice and Cranberry Salad

Wild rice is an aquatic grass with a nutty flavor and tender center that is a far cry from everyday white and brown rice. Cranberries, walnuts, and bitter greens are a tasty trifecta that will make this rice salad your new holiday standby.

SERVES 8
HANDS-ON 1 HOUR, 5 MINUTES
TOTAL 1 HOUR, 55 MINUTES

4   cups water
1   cup uncooked wild rice, rinsed
½   teaspoon table salt
2   cups (¾-inch) baguette cubes
2   tablespoons salted butter, melted
2   tablespoons shredded fresh Parmesan cheese
½   cup dried cranberries
⅓   cup chopped toasted walnuts
3   cups arugula (about 2 ounces)
1   cup torn radicchio (about 1½ ounces)
¼   cup olive oil
2   tablespoons Champagne vinegar
1   tablespoon minced shallot
½   teaspoon table salt
¼   teaspoon freshly ground black pepper

❶ Preheat oven to 400°F. Bring water, rice, and salt to a boil in a large saucepan over medium-high. Reduce heat to medium-low; cover and simmer until rice is tender and grains start to open, 50 to 55 minutes. Drain well; rinse rice under cold water, and drain again.

❷ Meanwhile, toss together baguette cubes, butter, and cheese in a medium bowl. Spread in a single layer on a parchment paper-lined baking sheet. Bake in preheated oven until toasted and golden, about 10 minutes. Remove from pan, and cool 10 minutes.

❸ Transfer rice to a large bowl; add cranberries and walnuts. Add arugula, radicchio, and croutons, tossing gently.

❹ Whisk together olive oil, vinegar, shallot, salt, and pepper; pour over salad, and toss gently to coat.

FRESH IDEA

Wild rice salads are a Christmas classic, but other grains that have a hearty, toothsome texture such as farro, pearl barley, or buckwheat are great substitutes. Just cook to package directions.

Green Beans with Brie Cream Sauce and Fried Shallots

Green beans are a holiday sideboard standard. Take them to new heights with a sauce enriched with Brie and the distinct crunch of fried shallots in place of the usual French fried onions.

SERVES 6
HANDS-ON 20 MINUTES
TOTAL 20 MINUTES

2   tablespoons salted butter
2   tablespoons all-purpose flour
1½   cups half-and-half
1   (8-ounce) Brie round, rind removed and cut into pieces
½   teaspoon table salt
1½   pounds fresh green beans, trimmed
½   cup vegetable oil
3   large shallots, thinly sliced (about 1 cup)
⅛   teaspoon freshly ground black pepper

❶ Melt butter in a medium saucepan over medium-low; whisk in flour. Gradually whisk in half-and-half. Increase heat to medium, and cook, whisking constantly, until thickened and bubbly. Remove from heat, and stir in Brie and ¼ teaspoon of the salt until smooth.

❷ Cook green beans in a small amount of boiling water until almost tender, 5 to 7 minutes; drain. Set aside, and keep warm.

❸ Heat oil in a medium-size, heavy saucepan or skillet (not nonstick) until very hot. Fry shallots, in 2 to 3 batches, until golden, 30 to 50 seconds, turning occasionally.

Drain on paper towels. Immediately sprinkle hot shallots with pepper and remaining ¼ teaspoon salt, tossing gently.

❹ Place green beans on a serving plate; drizzle with cheese sauce, and sprinkle with fried shallots.

Potatoes Anna with Caramelized Onion Gravy

This French potato cake will wow your guests. It's actually easy to make with a mandoline slicer or food processor blade.

SERVES 8
HANDS-ON 1 HOUR
TOTAL 2 HOURS, INCLUDING GRAVY

½   cup (4 ounces) salted butter
3   pounds russet potatoes, peeled and cut into ⅛-inch-thick slices
2   teaspoons kosher salt
½   teaspoon black pepper
Fresh flat-leaf parsley or thyme leaves (optional)
Caramelized Onion Gravy

❶ Preheat oven to 450°F. Melt 2 tablespoons of the butter in a 10-inch cast-iron skillet over medium. Starting in the center, arrange a single layer of potato slices, overlapping, in a circular pattern in skillet; sprinkle with about ⅜ teaspoon salt and about ⅛ teaspoon pepper. Brush with about 1 tablespoon butter. Repeat layers 4 more times, starting with potatoes and ending with butter. Press firmly to pack.

❷ Cover with aluminum foil, and bake in preheated oven 20 minutes. Uncover and bake until potatoes are browned on bottom, 30 to 35 minutes.

❸ Loosen edges of potatoes with a spatula. Place a plate upside down on top of skillet; invert potatoes onto plate. Garnish with parsley or thyme leaves, if desired, and serve with Caramelized Onion Gravy.

CARAMELIZED ONION GRAVY

3   tablespoons salted butter
2   medium Vidalia onions, cut into thin vertical slices (about 2 cups)
⅓   cup (about 2 ⅓ ounces) dry sherry
1½   tablespoons cornstarch
1½   cups chicken or turkey stock
2   teaspoons fresh thyme leaves
½   teaspoon table salt

❶ Melt butter in a large skillet with high sides or Dutch oven over medium-high. Add onions; cook, stirring often, 5 minutes. Reduce heat to medium, and cook, stirring often, until deep golden brown, about 25 minutes. Add sherry, and cook, stirring constantly, until liquid almost evaporates, 3 to 5 minutes.

❷ Stir together cornstarch and 2 tablespoons of the stock. Add cornstarch mixture to remaining stock, stirring constantly. Gradually add stock mixture, thyme, and salt to onion mixture in skillet, and cook over medium heat until bubbly and slightly thickened.

Note: Potatoes Anna can be made a day ahead, wrapped in foil, and refrigerated overnight. Reheat in skillet, uncovered, at 375°F for 20 minutes or until thoroughly heated. Gravy can be made a day ahead and reheated before serving.

Butter-Braised Celery

If braised celery is new to you, it will remind you of the caramelized, meltingly tender celery that comes from the pan drippings and veggies in a pot roast.

SERVES 4
HANDS-ON 30 MINUTES
TOTAL 30 MINUTES

1   (1½-pound) bunch celery with leaves
3   tablespoons (1½ ounces) salted butter
1½ cups chicken or turkey stock
1   tablespoon fresh lemon juice (from ½ lemon)
¼   teaspoon sea salt
1½ tablespoons roughly chopped fresh chives
¼   teaspoon black pepper

❶ Separate celery into stalks. Remove and reserve some of the leaves for garnish, if desired; keep remaining leaves attached. Using a vegetable peeler, remove the veins on exterior of celery stalks, and trim and discard about 1 inch from bottoms. Cut each stalk into about 2- x ½-inch pieces.

❷ Heat butter in a large skillet over medium-high until hot, about 2 minutes; add celery. Cook, stirring occasionally, until lightly browned, about 8 minutes. (Do not stir too often or celery won't brown. Much of the flavor will come from the caramelized browning.)

❸ Add chicken stock, lemon juice, and salt; bring to a boil. Cover; reduce heat to medium-low, and simmer, stirring occasionally, just until celery is tender-crisp, about 6 minutes. Uncover, increase heat to medium-high, and cook until celery is very tender and enough liquid evaporates to make a buttery sauce, 8 to 10 minutes. Transfer to a serving bowl; sprinkle with chives and pepper. Garnish with celery leaves, if desired.

Broccolini with Pancetta and Breadcrumbs

The pleasant bitterness of Broccolini, a hybrid of broccoli and kale, is tempered by salty pancetta.

SERVES 6
HANDS-ON 40 MINUTES
TOTAL 40 MINUTES

1½ pounds Broccolini
2½ ounces French bread, cut into cubes
6   tablespoons (3 ounces) salted butter
4   garlic cloves
1   tablespoon chopped fresh flat-leaf parsley
2   teaspoons chopped fresh chives
1   teaspoon chopped fresh sage
⅜   teaspoon kosher salt
¼   teaspoon black pepper
½   ounce Parmesan cheese, grated (about 2 tablespoons)
6   ounces thinly sliced pancetta, cut into thin strips

❶ Remove leaves from Broccolini; trim and discard about 1 inch off bottoms of stalks. Cut thickest stalks in half lengthwise, if necessary. Set Broccolini aside.

❷ Pulse bread cubes in a food processor until coarsely ground with some larger pieces remaining, about 12 times.

❸ Melt 3 tablespoons of the butter in a large nonstick skillet over medium. Mince 2 of the garlic cloves, and add with breadcrumbs to skillet. Cook, stirring often, until breadcrumb mixture is lightly browned and crisp, about 5 minutes. Stir in parsley, chives, sage, and ⅛ teaspoon each of the salt and pepper. Remove from heat; place in a bowl, and stir in Parmesan cheese.

❹ Wipe skillet clean. Place pancetta in skillet over medium, and cook, stirring often, until crisp, about 5 minutes. Remove from skillet using a slotted spoon, reserving drippings in skillet; drain pancetta on paper towels.

❺ Melt remaining 3 tablespoons butter in hot drippings over medium. Slice remaining 2 garlic cloves; add to skillet, and cook, stirring constantly, until lightly browned, about 2 minutes. Remove garlic from skillet, using a slotted spoon.

❻ Increase heat to medium-high, and add Broccolini to skillet. Cover and cook, tossing occasionally, until Broccolini is lightly browned in spots and stems are tender-crisp, 8 to 10 minutes. Return garlic slices to skillet, and add remaining ¼ teaspoon salt and ⅛ teaspoon pepper, tossing with Broccolini.

❼ Place Broccolini on a serving platter; sprinkle with herbed breadcrumbs and pancetta.

EARTHY DELIGHTS

Mushrooms have a rich flavor and fall into two categories: cultivated and wild. Cultivated mushrooms, like button or cremini, are readily available in supermarkets. The exotic flavors of wild mushrooms are prized by cooks and chefs. Unless you're an expert, it's safest to buy professionally foraged or cultivated wild varieties at specialty markets.

Mushroom Medley with Butter-Brandy Sauce and Parmesan

To brown mushrooms, turn up the heat and don't stir. Stirring too often too soon and over low heat sweats the mushrooms, hindering the browning process.

SERVES 8
HANDS-ON 30 MINUTES
TOTAL 30 MINUTES

2   **pounds combination of shiitake, portobello, and cremini mushrooms**
6   **tablespoons (3 ounces) salted butter**
4   **tablespoons olive oil**
1   **teaspoon kosher salt**
¼   **teaspoon black pepper**
⅔   **cup (about 5⅓ ounces) brandy**
1   **cup chicken stock**
1   **ounce Parmesan cheese, shaved (about ¼ cup)**
Fresh thyme leaves (optional)

❶ Remove and discard stems from shiitake mushrooms, and slice caps. Remove and discard stems and gills from portobello mushroom caps; cut each cap into 8 wedges. Quarter cremini mushrooms.

❷ Heat 2 tablespoons each of the butter and olive oil in a large skillet over medium-high, stirring until butter is melted and mixture is hot, about 2 minutes. Add half of the mushrooms, and cook, without stirring, until well browned on 1 side, 3 to 4 minutes. Stir mushrooms once, and cook, without stirring, 2 to 3 minutes. Stir once, and cook until mushrooms are well browned on all sides, about 2 minutes. Remove cooked mushrooms from skillet, and reserve. Repeat procedure with 2 tablespoons butter, remaining 2 tablespoons oil, and remaining half of uncooked mushrooms.

❸ Return reserved cooked mushrooms to skillet. Sprinkle mushrooms with salt and pepper, and stir in brandy. Cook, stirring constantly to loosen browned bits from bottom of skillet, until almost all liquid has evaporated, about 1 minute. Stir in chicken stock; cook until slightly thickened, about 4 minutes.

❹ Remove from heat; add remaining 2 tablespoons butter, stirring until butter melts. Transfer mushrooms to a serving bowl; sprinkle with shaved Parmesan cheese, and, if desired, garnish with thyme leaves.

GARDEN FRESH

A live Christmas tree brings joy to your home now and to your garden later. Branch out by decorating one of these unexpected options:

ALL-AMERICAN

Great for containers or planted in the ground after Christmas, an **American boxwood** requires just one trimming a year to maintain its shape.

SOCIAL CLIMBER

English ivy, trained on a wire frame, is suitable indoors with indirect light or outdoors in a shady spot in your garden. Periodic trimming keeps it the same size forever.

WINTER STAR

This dense, slow-growing tree—**'Red Star' white cedar**—gets its name from soft, star-shaped foliage that changes from blue-green to reddish-purple in cold weather.

GOLDEN GIRL

Soft sprays of golden foliage make the golden **Hinoki false cypress** stand out. Outdoors, it grows 50 feet tall and 25 feet wide and makes a tall screen.

Pumpkin Spice Cake with Caramel-
Sea Salt Frosting, Peppermint Swirl
Cheesecake, Eggnog Semifreddo

CLASSIC
desserts with a twist

We've taken the traditional Christmas desserts that are a fixture on holiday sideboards and given them a unique twist...or two, so that this year the familiar finishes to the holiday feast are anything but expected.

Merry Christmas Trifle

Spicy Chocolate Gingerbread
Bûche de Noël

Bananas Foster Bread Pudding, Dried Fruit-Brown Sugar Pound Cake with Orange Glaze

Pear. Cranberry. Rosemary Galette

Spicy Chocolate Gingerbread Bûche de Noël

Chocolate-covered gingerbread is a tasty update on the classic yule log.

SERVES 10
HANDS-ON 1 HOUR, 10 MINUTES
TOTAL 3 HOURS, 25 MINUTES

CAKE
- 5 large eggs, separated
- ½ cup molasses
- ¼ cup packed dark brown sugar
- 3 tablespoons minced crystallized ginger
- ½ cup (1⅞ ounces) cake flour
- ¼ cup unsweetened cocoa
- 1 teaspoon baking powder
- 1 teaspoon ground ginger
- ½ teaspoon ground cinnamon
- ¼ teaspoon ground nutmeg
- ¼ teaspoon table salt
- ⅓ cup granulated sugar

FILLING
- 1 (8-ounce) container mascarpone
- 1 cup heavy cream
- 1 teaspoon vanilla extract
- ⅓ cup powdered sugar
- ¼ teaspoon ground ginger
- ¼ teaspoon ground cinnamon
- ⅛ teaspoon ground nutmeg

MOCHA BUTTERCREAM FROSTING
- ⅓ cup (about 3 ounces) salted butter, softened
- 2 cups powdered sugar
- ⅓ cup unsweetened cocoa
- 2 tablespoons hot water
- 1 teaspoon instant espresso granules
- 1 teaspoon vanilla extract

❶ Prepare the Cake: Preheat oven to 325°F. Line a 17- x 12-inch rimmed baking sheet with parchment paper; lightly grease with cooking spray. Beat egg yolks with a heavy-duty electric stand mixer on high speed until thick and pale, about 2 minutes. Add molasses, brown sugar, and crystallized ginger; beat on medium speed just until combined. Whisk flour and next 6 ingredients in a small bowl until combined. Fold flour mixture into egg yolk mixture to combine.

❷ Beat egg whites with an electric mixer on high speed until foamy. Gradually add ¼ cup of the granulated sugar, and beat until stiff, glossy peaks form. Gently fold egg white mixture into batter until no streaks remain. Spread batter in prepared baking sheet, smoothing into an even layer and being careful not to deflate batter.

❸ Bake in preheated oven until lightly browned and a wooden pick inserted in center comes out clean, 14 to 16 minutes. Transfer baking sheet to a wire rack, and gently run a sharp knife around the cake edges to loosen. Sprinkle cake with remaining 1 tablespoon granulated sugar. Cool 5 minutes. Cover cake with a clean towel, and top with a large cutting board. Invert cake onto cutting board. Remove baking sheet, and carefully peel off and discard parchment. Cover loosely with a second clean towel, and roll cake up gently, using bottom towel to help roll, and cool completely, about 30 minutes.

❹ Prepare the Filling: Stir mascarpone cheese in a large bowl just until loosened. Beat cream and vanilla with an electric mixer on high speed until foamy. Gradually add powdered sugar, ginger, cinnamon, and nutmeg, beating on high speed until soft peaks form. Stir one-fourth of the whipped cream mixture into mascarpone using a rubber spatula; fold in remaining whipped cream mixture (be careful not to overmix or mixture will be grainy). Chill until ready to use.

❺ Prepare the Frosting: Beat butter on medium speed with an electric mixer until creamy. Whisk together powdered sugar and cocoa in a small bowl; gradually add cocoa mixture to butter, beating on medium-low speed until smooth. Stir together hot water and espresso granules until dissolved. Gradually add 1 tablespoon espresso mixture and vanilla, and beat until smooth; gradually add remaining espresso mixture, 1 teaspoon at a time, to reach desired consistency.

❻ Assemble the Bûche de Noël: Unroll cake, and remove towels. Spread Filling evenly over the entire surface of the cake. Starting at 1 short end, roll up cake, jelly roll-style. Wrap the roll tightly in plastic wrap, and chill until firm, about 2 hours.

❼ Unwrap cake roll, and discard plastic wrap. Cut a 2-inch slice on the bias from 1 short end of cake roll. (The slice will be a tree branch.) Spread 2 tablespoons of the Frosting on top and sides of small cake slice, leaving ends exposed. Attach straight side of small slice to 1 long side of cake roll. Spread Frosting on cake roll. Using a fork, draw lines in Frosting to resemble bark. Draw circles on cake ends to resemble tree rings. Cover and chill until ready to serve. Dust lightly with powdered sugar, if desired.

Dried Fruit-Brown Sugar Pound Cake with Orange Glaze

Reminiscent of Christmas fruitcake, bourbon-plumped fruit is encased in dense, moist pound cake with a delicate crumb.

SERVES 16

HANDS-ON 20 MINUTES

TOTAL 4 HOURS

½ cup dried cranberries
½ cup golden raisins
½ cup roughly chopped dried cherries
½ cup bourbon
1½ cups (12 ounces) salted butter, softened
1 (8-ounce) package cream cheese, softened
2 cups packed light brown sugar
1 cup granulated sugar
6 large eggs
3 cups (about 12¾ ounces) all-purpose flour
1 teaspoon baking powder
¾ teaspoon ground cinnamon
½ teaspoon table salt
¼ teaspoon ground nutmeg
¼ teaspoon ground allspice
1 cup chopped toasted pecans
1 tablespoon orange zest
1½ teaspoons vanilla extract
Orange Glaze

❶ Preheat oven to 325°F. Grease and flour a 10-inch tube pan.

❷ Combine cranberries, raisins, and cherries in a small microwave-safe bowl; stir in ¼ cup of the bourbon. Microwave on HIGH 1 minute, stirring after 30 seconds. Cool completely, stirring occasionally, about 15 minutes.

❸ Beat butter and cream cheese with a heavy-duty electric stand mixer on medium speed until creamy, about 2 minutes. Gradually add brown sugar and granulated sugar, beating until light and fluffy, about 4 minutes. Add eggs, 1 at a time, beating just until blended after each addition.

❹ Whisk together flour, baking powder, cinnamon, salt, nutmeg, and allspice in a bowl. With mixer running on low speed, add flour mixture to butter mixture alternately with remaining ¼ cup bourbon, beginning and ending with flour mixture, beating just until blended after each addition. Stir in pecans, orange zest, vanilla, and cranberry mixture. Pour batter into prepared pan.

❺ Bake in preheated oven until a wooden pick inserted in center of cake comes out clean, about 1½ hours. Cool in pan on a wire rack 10 minutes. Invert cake onto rack; cool completely, about 2 hours. Transfer cake to a serving platter. Spoon Orange Glaze over cake.

Orange Glaze: Stir together 2 cups powdered sugar, 3 tablespoons fresh orange juice, 2 teaspoons orange zest, and ½ teaspoon vanilla extract until smooth.

Eggnog Semifreddo

Enjoy the classic flavor of spiked eggnog in frozen form.

SERVES 6

HANDS-ON 35 MINUTES

TOTAL 12 HOURS, 40 MINUTES, INCLUDING 12 HOURS FREEZING

20 ladyfingers
½ cup granulated sugar
¼ cup bourbon
4 large egg yolks
2 teaspoons vanilla extract
¼ teaspoon kosher salt
¼ teaspoon ground nutmeg, plus more for garnish
2¼ cups whipping cream
5 tablespoons powdered sugar

❶ Lightly grease a 9- x 5-inch loaf pan. Line pan with plastic wrap, allowing 4 inches to extend over sides. Line bottom and sides of pan with ladyfingers, standing up vertically around sides of pan.

❷ Fill a saucepan with 1 inch of water; bring to a boil over medium-high. Set a large metal bowl on saucepan. Combine sugar, bourbon, egg yolks, vanilla, and salt in bowl. Whisk until mixture thickens and a candy thermometer registers 160°F. Remove from heat; cool 5 minutes. Beat with an electric mixer on medium until mixture doubles in volume, 3 minutes. Stir in nutmeg.

❸ Beat 1¾ cups of the cream on medium-high until foamy; gradually add 3 tablespoons of the powdered sugar until stiff peaks form. Fold whipped cream into sugar mixture. Spoon into prepared pan; smooth top. Fold excess plastic wrap over top to cover. Freeze 12 to 24 hours.

❹ Beat remaining ½ cup cream on medium-high speed until foamy. Gradually add remaining 2 tablespoons powdered sugar; beat until soft peaks form. Chill.

❺ Transfer frozen semifreddo onto serving platter. Remove and discard plastic wrap. Let stand 15 minutes. Just before serving, top with whipped cream. Garnish with a light sprinkling of nutmeg, if desired.

Merry Christmas Trifle

The pound cake in this trifle soaks up the rum and pineapple syrup to become creamy in texture.

SERVES 12
HANDS-ON 30 MINUTES
TOTAL 3 HOURS, 30 MINUTES

1   (20-ounce) can pineapple chunks in syrup, undrained
1   (16-ounce) container fresh strawberries, hulled and quartered
⅓   cup coconut-flavored rum
1   (16-ounce) frozen pound cake, thawed and cut into 1-inch cubes
3   bananas, sliced
Coconut Cream Custard
1   cup sweetened coconut flakes, toasted, plus more for garnish
1   cup heavy cream
¼   cup powdered sugar
½   teaspoon vanilla extract
¼   cup toasted slivered almonds

❶ Stir together pineapple, strawberries, and rum in a medium bowl. Cover and chill 20 minutes. Remove fruit from bowl with a slotted spoon, reserving syrup. Place half of cake cubes in bottom of a trifle dish. Drizzle with half of reserved fruit syrup. Top with half of pineapple mixture, half of banana slices, half of the custard, and half of toasted coconut. Repeat layers.

❷ Beat heavy cream with an electric mixer on medium speed until foamy; gradually add powdered sugar and vanilla, beating until soft peaks form. Dollop whipped cream over top of trifle. Sprinkle with almonds. Garnish with toasted coconut, if desired.

COCONUT CREAM CUSTARD

1   cup granulated sugar
⅓   cup cornstarch
2   cups whole milk
1   (14-ounce) can coconut milk
6   large egg yolks
1   tablespoon coconut-flavored rum
1   teaspoon vanilla extract

Whisk together sugar and cornstarch in a large saucepan. Whisk together milk, coconut milk, and egg yolks in a bowl. Whisk milk mixture into sugar mixture. Bring to a boil over medium, whisking constantly; cook, whisking constantly, until thickened. Remove from heat, and whisk in rum and vanilla. Place plastic wrap directly on custard (to prevent a film from forming). Cool 1 hour. Cover and chill until cold, about 2 hours.

Pear, Cranberry, Rosemary Galette

Southern cheese wafers inspire this unique galette crust.

SERVES 8
HANDS-ON 25 MINUTES
TOTAL 4 HOURS, 15 MINUTES, INCLUDING 2 HOURS CHILLING

CRUST
2   cups (about 8½ ounces) all-purpose flour
½   cup chopped toasted pecans
1   teaspoon granulated sugar
½   teaspoon table salt
4   ounces sharp white Cheddar cheese, finely shredded
¾   cup (6 ounces) cold salted butter, cut into small cubes
5 to 6 tablespoons ice water

GALETTE
2   pounds firm, ripe Bartlett pears, peeled, cored, and sliced
1   cup fresh cranberries
½   cup firmly packed brown sugar
3   tablespoons all-purpose flour
1   teaspoon chopped fresh rosemary
1   teaspoon vanilla extract
¼   teaspoon table salt
1   large egg, lightly beaten
3   tablespoons Demerara sugar

❶ Prepare the Crust: Process flour, pecans, granulated sugar, and salt in a food processor until finely ground, 15 seconds. Add Cheddar and butter; pulse 6 times until mixture resembles coarse meal. While pulsing, drizzle 5 to 6 tablespoons ice water over mixture until clumps form. Turn out onto a work surface and form into a 1-inch-thick disk. Wrap in plastic wrap; chill 2 hours.

❷ Prepare the Galette: Preheat oven to 400°F. Gently stir together pears, cranberries, brown sugar, flour, rosemary, vanilla, and salt in a large bowl. (Do not make filling ahead of time; it will become too juicy.)

❸ Unwrap chilled dough, and place on floured parchment paper; sprinkle with flour, and top with a second piece of parchment paper. Roll into a 15-inch circle. Remove top piece of parchment paper; transfer dough and bottom piece of parchment paper to a baking sheet. Spoon pear mixture into center of dough circle, leaving a 2½-inch border. Fold edges of dough up and over filling (leaving an opening at center), pleating as you go and sealing any cracks. Brush dough with beaten egg, and sprinkle dough and fruit with Demerara sugar.

❹ Bake until crust is golden brown, pears are tender, and juices are thickened in the center, about 50 minutes, shielding crust edges with aluminum foil to prevent overbrowning. Remove pan to a wire rack; cool 1 hour.

Pumpkin Spice Cake with Caramel-Sea Salt Frosting

Traditional pumpkin pie morphs into an impressive layer cake that is sure to be a new holiday favorite.

SERVES 12
HANDS-ON 30 MINUTES
TOTAL 1 HOUR, 40 MINUTES

Shortening
1   cup (8 ounces) salted butter, softened
1   cup granulated sugar
1   cup packed light brown sugar
4   large eggs
1¼ cups canned pumpkin
2   teaspoons vanilla extract
3   cups (about 12¾ ounces) all-purpose flour
1   tablespoon baking powder
½   teaspoon baking soda
½   teaspoon table salt
2   teaspoons ground cinnamon
1   teaspoon ground ginger
½   teaspoon ground nutmeg
1   cup buttermilk
Caramel-Sea Salt Frosting
Flaked sea salt

❶ Prepare the Cake: Preheat oven to 350°F. Grease (with shortening) and flour 2 (9-inch) round cake pans.

❷ Beat butter with a heavy-duty electric stand mixer on medium until creamy. Gradually add granulated and brown sugar; beat until light and fluffy. Add eggs, 1 at a time, beating until blended after each addition. Add pumpkin and vanilla, and beat just until blended.

❸ Stir together flour, baking powder, baking soda, salt, cinnamon, ginger, and nutmeg. Add to butter mixture alternately with buttermilk, beginning and ending with flour mixture, beating on low speed just until blended after each addition. Spoon batter into prepared cake pans.

❹ Bake in preheated oven until a wooden pick inserted in center comes out clean, 30 to 40 minutes. Cool in pans on a wire rack 10 minutes; remove cakes from pans to wire rack, and cool completely, about 30 minutes.

❺ Spread Caramel-Sea Salt Frosting on top of 1 cake layer. Top with second cake layer. Spread frosting on top and sides of cake. Sprinkle with flaked sea salt.

CARAMEL-SEA SALT FROSTING

MAKES ABOUT 3½ CUPS

1   cup (8 ounces) salted butter
1   cup packed light brown sugar
1   cup packed dark brown sugar
1   tablespoon light corn syrup
½   cup heavy cream
4   cups powdered sugar
2   teaspoons vanilla extract
¼   teaspoon sea salt

Combine butter, light brown sugar, dark brown sugar, and corn syrup in a 3½-quart saucepan. Bring to a boil over medium, stirring constantly. Stir in cream, and return to a boil, stirring constantly; remove from heat. Pour mixture into bowl of a heavy-duty electric stand mixer fitted with the whisk attachment. With mixer running on medium speed, gradually add powdered sugar, vanilla, and salt; beat until thickened and spreadable, 8 to 10 minutes. Use immediately.

Bananas Foster Bread Pudding

Serve up a New Orleans' classic in bread pudding form. Wrap up the extra loaf of bread to give.

SERVES 6
HANDS-ON 40 MINUTES
TOTAL 3 HOURS, 15 MINUTES

BANANA BREAD

1   cup (8 ounces) salted butter, softened
¾   cup granulated sugar
¾   cup packed light brown sugar
3   large eggs
¼   cup sour cream
1   teaspoon vanilla extract
3¼   cups all-purpose flour
¾   teaspoon ground cinnamon
¾   teaspoon baking powder
¾   teaspoon baking soda
¾   teaspoon table salt
¼   teaspoon ground nutmeg
2½   cups mashed ripe bananas
1   cup chopped toasted pecans

BREAD PUDDING

1   Banana Bread loaf, cubed
4   large eggs
½   cup granulated sugar
¼   teaspoon table salt
¼   teaspoon ground cinnamon
2   cups whole milk
1½   cups heavy cream
2   tablespoons rum

RUM HARD SAUCE

½   cup (4 ounces) salted butter, softened
2   tablespoons rum
1½   cups powdered sugar
1   teaspoon vanilla extract

❶ Prepare the Banana Bread: Preheat oven to 350°F. Lightly grease 2 (8- x 4-inch) loaf pans.

❷ Beat butter with a heavy-duty electric stand mixer on medium until creamy, about 2 minutes. Add sugars; beat until light and fluffy, about 4 minutes. Add eggs, 1 at a time, beating just until blended after each. Add sour cream and vanilla; beat just until blended.

❸ Stir together flour and next 5 ingredients. Gradually add flour mixture to butter mixture, beating on low. Stir in bananas and pecans. Spoon into prepared pans.

❹ Bake in preheated oven until a wooden pick inserted in center comes out clean, about 1 hour. Cool in pans on a wire rack 10 minutes. Remove from pans, and cool completely on rack, about 1 hour.

❺ Prepare the Bread Pudding: Preheat oven to 400°F. Spread Banana Bread cubes in a lightly greased jelly-roll pan. Bake until lightly toasted, 15 minutes. Transfer to a wire rack; cool 15 minutes. Reduce oven temperature to 350°F.

❻ Whisk together eggs, sugar, salt, and cinnamon in a large bowl until well blended. Whisk in milk, cream, and rum until well blended. Gently stir toasted bread cubes into egg mixture until coated. Let stand 20 minutes. Spread mixture in a lightly greased 11- x 7-inch baking dish.

❼ Bake at 350°F until set in center, about 1 hour, shielding with aluminum foil after 45 minutes to prevent excessive browning, if necessary. Cool 15 minutes.

❽ While Bread Pudding cools, prepare the Rum Hard Sauce: Beat butter and rum with an electric mixer on medium speed until creamy, 1 minute. Gradually add powdered sugar and vanilla, beating until fluffy. Serve immediately with warm Bread Pudding.

Peppermint Swirl Cheesecake

SERVES 12

HANDS-ON 35 MINUTES

TOTAL 11 HOURS, 37 MINUTES, INCLUDING 8 HOURS CHILLING

CRUST

2 **cups chocolate wafer crumbs (about 35 wafers)**

5 **tablespoons butter, melted**

3 **tablespoons granulated sugar**

FILLING

4 **(8-ounce) packages cream cheese, softened**

1 **cup granulated sugar**

4 **large eggs**

1 **teaspoon vanilla extract**

½ **teaspoon peppermint extract**

¼ **cup crushed peppermint candies**

GANACHE

1 **(4-ounce) semisweet chocolate baking bar, finely chopped**

1 **(4-ounce) dark chocolate baking bar, finely chopped**

1 **cup heavy cream**

¼ **teaspoon peppermint extract**

ADDITIONAL INGREDIENT
Crushed peppermint candies

❶ Prepare the Crust: Preheat oven to 350°F. Stir together all Crust ingredients in a medium bowl. Press mixture on bottom and 1 inch up sides of a lightly greased 9-inch round springform pan. Bake 10 minutes. Let stand at room temperature until ready to use.

❷ Prepare the Filling: Reduce oven temperature to 325°F. Beat cream cheese with a heavy-duty electric stand mixer on medium until smooth, 1½ minutes. Gradually add sugar, beating just until blended. Add eggs, 1 at a time, beating just until incorporated after each. Beat in vanilla and peppermint extract.

❸ Transfer 1 cup of the cheesecake batter to a small bowl; stir in crushed peppermint candies just until mixture turns pink.

❹ Pour about two-thirds of plain cheesecake batter into prepared crust; dollop the peppermint candy batter over batter in pan, and gently swirl with a knife. Spoon remaining plain batter into pan, and smooth with an offset spatula or a knife.

❺ Bake at 325°F just until center is set, 1 hour to 1 hour and 5 minutes. Turn oven off. Let cheesecake stand in oven, with door closed, 15 minutes. Remove cheesecake from oven, and gently run a knife around outer edge of cheesecake to loosen from sides of pan. (Do not remove sides of pan.) Cool completely in pan on a wire rack, about 1 hour. Cover and chill 8 to 24 hours.

❻ Prepare the Ganache: Combine semisweet chocolate and dark chocolate in a small heatproof bowl. Heat cream in a small saucepan over low just until bubbles appear around edges of pan. Pour warm cream over chocolate in bowl, and let stand 1 minute. Stir until smooth and melted; stir in peppermint extract. Let stand until slightly warm, 15 to 20 minutes.

❼ Remove sides and bottom of springform pan, and place cheesecake on a serving plate. Slowly pour slightly warm Ganache over cheesecake, spreading to edges. Chill 1 hour before serving. Garnish with additional crushed peppermint candies, if desired.

Potato, Radish, and Brussels Sprouts Frittata;
Savory Sausage, Mushroom, and Greens Bread
Pudding; Bourbon-Pecan Sweet Potato Bread

BESTOVERS

*After hours of planning, cooking, greeting, eating, and then bidding guests
farewell, the last thing you want to do is throw out all the delicious leftovers.
So don't! We've come up with some great new dishes built around what's left.*

Smoked Pork Tenderloin Sliders
with Brussels Sprouts Slaw

Beer-Braised Beef Short Rib
Ragu over Pappardelle

Potato, Radish, and Brussels Sprouts Frittata

A comforting crustless quiche is a terrific way to use up leftover vegetable sides.

SERVES 8
HANDS-ON 10 MINUTES
TOTAL 25 MINUTES

12   large eggs
½   cup whipping cream
1   teaspoon kosher salt
½   teaspoon black pepper
4   ounces Havarti cheese, shredded (about 1 cup)
2   tablespoons olive oil
1½   cups leftover Fingerling Potatoes with Picholine Olives and Shallots (page 80)
1½   cups leftover Roasted Brussels Sprouts and Radishes with Lemon Vinaigrette (page 79)
2   tablespoons coarsely chopped fresh flat-leaf parsley

❶ Preheat oven to 375°F. Whisk together eggs, cream, salt, and pepper in a medium bowl. Stir in ½ cup of the cheese.

❷ Heat oil in a 10-inch well-seasoned cast-iron skillet or 10-inch ovenproof nonstick skillet over medium. Add leftover vegetables to pan; cook until warmed through, about 3 minutes. Pour egg mixture over vegetables in pan, shaking pan to evenly distribute vegetables. Cook, without stirring, until the edges begin to set, about 5 minutes. Sprinkle with remaining ½ cup cheese.

❸ Bake in preheated oven until top is golden brown and center is just set, 12 to 15 minutes. Sprinkle with parsley before serving.

FRESH IDEA

Waste not, want not. Stir leftover, wilted salads and slaws into soups or hot pasta or rice for an extra serving of vegetables. Leftover cooked mushrooms can be processed with pitted olives, citrus zest, herbs, and olive oil for a zesty tapenade. Meats can be sliced or shredded to fill tacos or lettuce wraps, or rolled into enchiladas and smothered in sauce and cheese.

Bourbon-Pecan Sweet Potato Bread

Everybody's favorite holiday mash lends moist sweetness to this bread.

SERVES 8
HANDS-ON 10 MINUTES
TOTAL 3 HOURS, 20 MINUTES

1½   cups (about 6 ⅜ ounces) all-purpose flour
1   teaspoon baking soda
¾   teaspoon ground cinnamon
½   teaspoon ground ginger
½   teaspoon baking powder
½   teaspoon table salt
½   cup candied pecans leftover from Bourbon-Pecan Mashed Sweet Potatoes (page 129), chopped (or use chopped toasted pecans)
1   cup leftover Bourbon-Pecan Mashed Sweet Potatoes (page 129)
¾   cup granulated sugar
½   cup canola oil
¼   cup whole milk
2   tablespoons bourbon
2   large eggs

SHARE A DISH

While there is nothing wrong with a disposable aluminum pan for sharing holiday leftovers, inexpensive serveware abounds these days. Match the type of container to the dish.

Nowadays you can find multiuse compostable containers made of bamboo, palm leaves, even sugarcane. These are terrific options when no reheating is required, and they look good, too.

1 Preheat oven to 350°F. Grease and flour an 8- x 4-inch loaf pan.

2 Whisk together flour, baking soda, cinnamon, ginger, baking powder, and salt in a large bowl. Stir in pecans.

3 In a separate bowl, whisk together sweet potatoes, sugar, oil, milk, bourbon, and eggs. Add sweet potato mixture to flour mixture; stir until just blended and dry ingredients are moistened. Pour batter into prepared pan.

4 Bake in preheated oven until a wooden pick inserted in center comes out clean, about 1 hour. Cool in pan 10 minutes; remove from pan, and cool completely on a wire rack, about 2 hours.

Savory Sausage, Mushroom, and Greens Bread Pudding

Untouched bread is often left to dry out, then whirled into breadcrumbs in a food processor. Here day-old dinner rolls become a casual meal—a one-dish, savory bread pudding that's anything but stale.

SERVES 8
HANDS-ON 15 MINUTES
TOTAL 1 HOUR, 30 MINUTES

10 leftover Herbed Yeast Spoon Rolls (page 62) (6½ cups loosely packed cubed rolls)
8 ounces bulk sweet Italian sausage
¼ cup (2 ounces) salted butter
1 cup chopped yellow onion

¾ cup thinly sliced celery
2 teaspoons minced garlic
1 (8-ounce) package sliced cremini mushrooms
1 teaspoon kosher salt
½ teaspoon black pepper
5 cups chopped Lacinato kale
1 cup chicken stock
1 cup heavy cream
4 large eggs

1 Preheat oven to 375°F. Grease an 11- x 7-inch (2-quart) baking dish.

2 Tear rolls into 1-inch pieces, and spread on a large rimmed baking sheet. Bake in preheated oven until golden and edges are crisp, stirring occasionally, about 20 minutes. Cool completely on pan, about 10 to 15 minutes.

3 Meanwhile, cook sausage in a large skillet over medium-high until browned, stirring frequently to crumble, about 6 minutes. Drain on a paper towel-lined plate; discard drippings in skillet.

4 Melt butter in same skillet over medium-high. Add onion and celery; cook until onion is tender, about 5 minutes. Add garlic and mushrooms, and sprinkle with ½ teaspoon of the salt and ¼ teaspoon of the pepper; cook until mushrooms are browned and celery is tender, about 8 minutes. Add kale; cook until wilted, about 2 minutes. Remove from heat, and stir in reserved sausage.

5 Whisk together chicken stock, cream, eggs, remaining ½ teaspoon salt, and remaining ¼ teaspoon pepper. Add bread and sausage mixture; stir gently until combined. Spoon mixture into prepared baking dish. Bake in preheated oven until set and golden brown, about 30 minutes.

Smoked Pork Tenderloin Sliders with Brussels Sprouts Slaw

Slices of pork tenderloin are the perfect diameter for sandwiching in a slider bun or roll. The cool-season slaw, made from tender Brussels sprouts, spiked with cider vinegar, mustard, and honey, is like a fresh take on traditional chowchow.

SERVES 4
HANDS-ON 15 MINUTES
TOTAL 15 MINUTES

1 pound Brussels sprouts, trimmed
¼ cup mayonnaise
1 tablespoon whole-grain Dijon mustard
2 teaspoons apple cider vinegar
1 teaspoon honey
½ teaspoon kosher salt
¼ teaspoon black pepper
8 (1.5-ounce) frozen yeast dinner rolls (such as Sister Schubert's)
½ cup jarred cranberry chutney or relish
16 (¼-inch) slices (about 1 ounce per slice) leftover Smoked Pork Tenderloins (page 45), warmed, if desired

1 Cut Brussels sprouts in half lengthwise; place cut sides down, and thinly slice crosswise. Whisk together mayonnaise, mustard, vinegar, honey, salt, and pepper in a medium bowl; add shredded Brussels sprouts, and toss to coat.

2 Heat rolls according to package directions; split. Spread cranberry chutney on bottoms of split rolls; top evenly with pork, Brussels sprouts slaw, and roll tops.

PUT YOUR FEET UP

The holiday feast is finished, gifts have been opened, and thank yous have been written. It's time to relax and reflect. Calling leftovers into service gives the cook a break. Let your family serve themselves when hunger strikes and enjoy the meal in an easy chair by the fire with a book in hand, or make it a movie night and eat while enjoying *It's a Wonderful Life*.

Beer-Braised Beef Short Rib Ragù over Pappardelle

Tender beef from one long, slow braise begets another luscious meal in less than half the time it would typically take. This dish is company-worthy if you dare to share.

SERVES 4
HANDS-ON 15 MINUTES
TOTAL 25 MINUTES

¼   cup (2 ounces) salted butter
1   cup chopped onion
1   (8-ounce) package sliced cremini mushrooms
2   teaspoons minced garlic
1   teaspoon kosher salt
½   teaspoon black pepper
2   cups reserved leftover cooking liquid from Beer-Braised Beef Short Ribs (page 123)

1 ½   cups coarsely shredded leftover Beer-Braised Beef Short Ribs (page 123)
1   cup finely chopped tomatoes, such as Pomì (from a 26.46-ounce container)
1   cup reserved leftover carrots from Beer-Braised Beef Short Ribs (page 123)
12   ounces uncooked pappardelle pasta
Fresh thyme leaves
Shaved Parmigiano-Reggiano cheese

❶ Melt 2 tablespoons of the butter in a large skillet over medium-high. Add onion, and cook, stirring often, until onion is softened, about 5 minutes. Add mushrooms and garlic; sprinkle with salt and pepper, and cook, stirring occasionally, until mushrooms are browned, about 8 minutes. Add reserved leftover cooking liquid, and cook, stirring constantly, to loosen browned bits from bottom of skillet.

❷ Stir in shredded beef, tomatoes, and carrots. Reduce heat to medium-low, and simmer, uncovered, stirring occasionally, until slightly thickened and beef and carrots are warmed through, about 5 minutes. Stir in remaining 2 tablespoons butter, and keep mixture warm.

❸ Cook pasta according to package directions; drain. Divide pasta among shallow serving bowls; top with ragù. Sprinkle with thyme and cheese.

FRESH IDEA

Short ribs are the starring ingredient of osso buco, a classic Italian braise. The dish is typically finished with gremolata, a mixture of minced flat-leaf parsley, finely grated lemon zest, and minced fresh garlic. Gremolata is a bright, bold flavor combo that is great on almost any grilled, braised, or roasted meat. It's also delicious mixed into softened butter to make a flavorful compound butter. A pat or two elevates a baked potato or steak to star status.

THAT'S A WRAP

Whether it's food or a unique find you're giving, match the package to the recipient's personal style for double the appreciation.

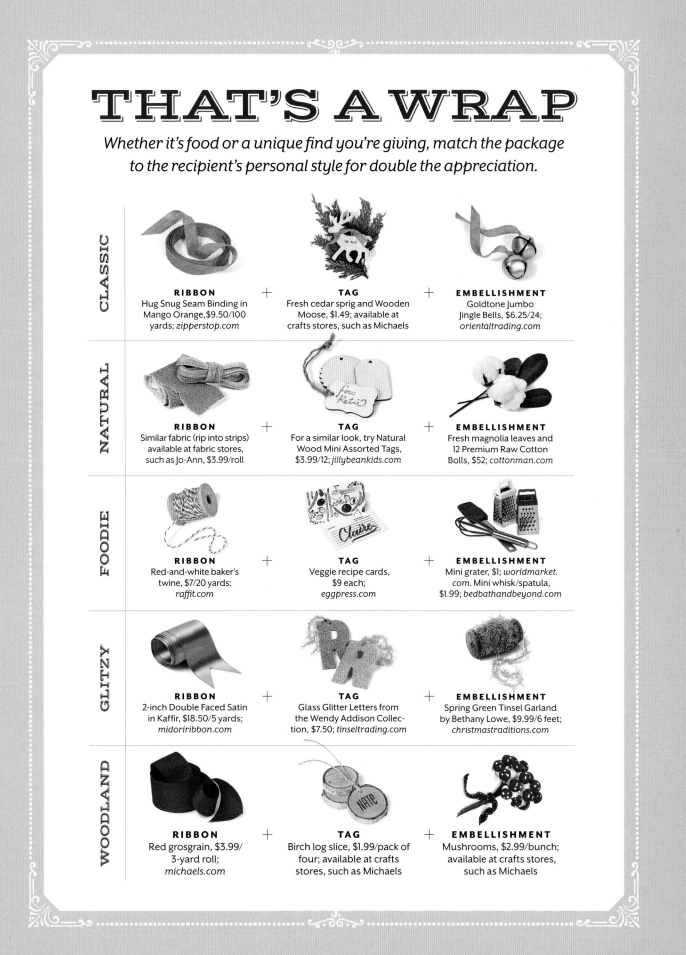

CLASSIC

RIBBON
Hug Snug Seam Binding in Mango Orange, $9.50/100 yards; *zipperstop.com*

+

TAG
Fresh cedar sprig and Wooden Moose, $1.49; available at crafts stores, such as Michaels

+

EMBELLISHMENT
Goldtone Jumbo Jingle Bells, $6.25/24; *orientaltrading.com*

NATURAL

RIBBON
Similar fabric (rip into strips) available at fabric stores, such as Jo-Ann, $3.99/roll

+

TAG
For a similar look, try Natural Wood Mini Assorted Tags, $3.99/12; *jillybeankids.com*

+

EMBELLISHMENT
Fresh magnolia leaves and 12 Premium Raw Cotton Bolls, $52; *cottonman.com*

FOODIE

RIBBON
Red-and-white baker's twine, $7/20 yards; *raffit.com*

+

TAG
Veggie recipe cards, $9 each; *eggpress.com*

+

EMBELLISHMENT
Mini grater, $1; *worldmarket. com.* Mini whisk/spatula, $1.99; *bedbathandbeyond.com*

GLITZY

RIBBON
2-inch Double Faced Satin in Kaffir, $18.50/5 yards; *midoriribbon.com*

+

TAG
Glass Glitter Letters from the Wendy Addison Collection, $7.50; *tinseltrading.com*

+

EMBELLISHMENT
Spring Green Tinsel Garland by Bethany Lowe, $9.99/6 feet; *christmastraditions.com*

WOODLAND

RIBBON
Red grosgrain, $3.99/ 3-yard roll; *michaels.com*

+

TAG
Birch log slice, $1.99/pack of four; available at crafts stores, such as Michaels

+

EMBELLISHMENT
Mushrooms, $2.99/bunch; available at crafts stores, such as Michaels

SHARE

ALL JARRED UP

During this season of giving, make something from the heart in the kitchen that your friends and loved ones will savor for days to come. Twist the lid, tie the bow, add a tag and you're good to go!

Bourbon Butter Pecan Sauce, Thyme-Lemon Curd,
Spiced-and-Spiked Chocolate Mousse

Roasted Garlic Tapenade, Herb-Marinated Mozzarella, Meyer Lemon-Cranberry Compound Butter

Ginger Pickled Pears,
Blood Orange Shrub Mix

THE RECIPES

④ Pour into 8 (8-ounce) jars; cool, uncovered, to room temperature, about 1 hour. Cover with lids, and chill up to 2 weeks. Serve with pecan sandies.

HOLIDAY HELPER

Stock up on interesting jars from brands such as Ball or Weck. Look for jars in pretty hues or pressed patterns for festive giving that's anything but ordinary.

Bourbon Butter Pecan Sauce

Three Southern favorites—smoky bourbon, rich butter, and earthy pecans—come together in a dessert sauce that will make the recipient swoon. It's also delicious stirred into a cup of dark roast coffee, spooned atop a piece of chocolate pie, or spread on a piece of toast with your afternoon tea. Be sure to include instructions for reheating on the gift.

MAKES 2 CUPS

HANDS-ON 11 MINUTES

TOTAL 2 HOURS, 21 MINUTES, INCLUDING 2 HOURS CHILLING

1   cup packed light brown sugar
½   cup (4 ounces) salted butter
½   cup heavy cream
⅛   teaspoon table salt
1   cup chopped toasted pecans
2   tablespoons bourbon

❶ Bring brown sugar, butter, cream, and salt to a boil in a small saucepan over medium, stirring constantly. Boil, stirring constantly, 1 minute. Remove from heat, and stir in pecans and bourbon. Pour evenly into 2 (8-ounce) jars, and cool 10 minutes. Cover with lids, and chill 2 hours or until ready to use.

❷ Reheat sauce in saucepan over medium-low, or microwave in jar with lid removed on HIGH 30 seconds. Stir sauce, and microwave 30 more seconds. Serve over ice cream.

Thyme-Lemon Curd

Citrus loves herbs and thyme is a delicious pairing here, but let your tastes guide you. Rosemary, lavender, or marjoram are other herbs that would work equally well.

MAKES 7½ CUPS

HANDS-ON 50 MINUTES

TOTAL 3 DAYS, 1 HOUR, 50 MINUTES, INCLUDING 3 DAYS STANDING

3   cups granulated sugar
10   thyme sprigs
12   large eggs, at room temperature
1½   cups fresh lemon juice (from 9 large lemons)
1   tablespoon lemon zest
2   cups (1 pound) salted butter, cubed

❶ Combine sugar and thyme sprigs in a medium-size airtight container. Let stand at room temperature 3 to 5 days, shaking occasionally.

❷ Remove and discard thyme sprigs. Fill bottom of a large double boiler with 2 inches of water; bring to a boil over medium-high. Reduce heat to medium-low, and simmer.

❸ Whisk eggs in top of double boiler off heat until well beaten. Gradually whisk in thyme-infused sugar, juice, and zest until well combined. Place top of double boiler over simmering water; add butter pieces. Cook, whisking constantly, until mixture thickens, about 25 minutes. Pour mixture through a fine wire-mesh strainer, pressing with a spoon to extract smooth curd. Discard solids.

Spiced-and-Spiked Chocolate Mousse

Because these must be kept chilled, they make a great hostess gift. You can ensure that they stay cold. The flavors of cinnamon and almond from the amaretto are natural with chocolate, but don't overlook the dash of cayenne. It adds a hint of heat and, as a pinch of salt does with sweets, really brings together the flavors.

MAKES 4 CUPS

HANDS-ON 12 MINUTES

TOTAL 1 HOUR, 12 MINUTES

¾   cup dark chocolate chips
¾   cup semisweet chocolate chips
½   teaspoon ground cinnamon
⅛   teaspoon cayenne pepper

1½ cups heavy cream
1½ tablespoons amaretto (almond liqueur)
1 teaspoon vanilla extract
2 tablespoons superfine sugar

① Microwave chocolate chips in a medium-size microwave-safe glass bowl on MEDIUM until melted and smooth, 1 minute and 30 seconds to 2 minutes, stirring every 30 seconds. Stir in cinnamon and cayenne. Cool 10 minutes.

② Beat cream, amaretto, and vanilla with a heavy-duty electric stand mixer on medium speed until foamy. Gradually add sugar, beating until soft peaks form.

③ Stir one-third of the whipped cream into chocolate mixture until smooth. Gradually fold in remaining whipped cream just until incorporated. Spoon or pipe mousse into 8 (4-ounce) jars. Cover with lids, and chill 1 hour or up to 2 days.

FRESH IDEA

Assemble a gift basket! A jar of from-scratch deliciousness is a welcome gift any time of year. Make it extra special by combining your food gift with the perfect accompaniments for the recipient to enjoy it. Package marinated cheese or tapenade with a loaf of artisan bread or crackers, a small wooden cutting board, and a knife for spreading. Chocolate mousse is terrific paired with a pound of espresso coffee and a pair of demitasse cups with spoons. Let your imagination guide you.

Herb-Marinated Mozzarella

Prepare these as an ideal, bite-sized appetizer to serve with a tray of olives and pickles or to use as a garnish atop salads. Keep chilled.

MAKES 2 CUPS
HANDS-ON 9 MINUTES
TOTAL 1 DAY, 9 MINUTES, INCLUDING 1 DAY CHILLING

4   (3-inch) rosemary sprigs
2   (2-inch) lemon peel strips
8   ounces fresh small mozzarella cheese balls, drained
¼   cup roughly chopped fresh flat-leaf parsley
1   tablespoon chopped fresh oregano
1   tablespoon chopped fresh thyme
1   teaspoon crushed red pepper
¼   teaspoon kosher salt
1   cup extra-virgin olive oil

Place rosemary sprigs and lemon peel strips in 2 (8-ounce) jars. Combine mozzarella, parsley, oregano, thyme, crushed red pepper, and salt; divide evenly between jars. Pour ½ cup olive oil in each jar, leaving ½-inch headspace. Cover and chill 1 day or up to 1 week. Serve cheese and infused oil on salads.

Roasted Garlic Tapenade

The lingering bite of fresh garlic you'd expect is tamed by swapping raw garlic for the sweetness of caramelized, roasted cloves.

MAKES ABOUT 1 CUP
HANDS-ON 16 MINUTES
TOTAL 16 MINUTES

1   garlic head
3   tablespoons olive oil
1   cup pitted kalamata olives
½   cup pitted Castelvetrano olives
1   tablespoon capers, drained
2   anchovy fillets
2   tablespoons chopped fresh flat-leaf parsley
1   tablespoon chopped fresh basil
1   tablespoon fresh lemon juice

① Preheat oven to 425°F. Peel and discard a few of the papery outer layers of the garlic head, leaving a few intact. Cut off pointed end of garlic head; place garlic on a piece of aluminum foil. Drizzle with ½ tablespoon of the oil, and fold foil to seal. Bake in preheated oven until garlic is softened, about 30 minutes; open top of foil pouch, and cool 15 minutes. Remove 3 garlic cloves from head, and peel; reserve remaining cloves for another use.

② Combine olives, capers, anchovies, and 3 peeled garlic cloves on a cutting board; coarsely chop. Stir together olive mixture, parsley, basil, lemon juice, and remaining 2 ½ tablespoons oil in a small bowl. Store in airtight jars in refrigerator up to 1 week. Serve with crudités or on goat cheese-smeared crostini.

Meyer Lemon-Cranberry Compound Butter

Winter citrus and holiday cranberries collide in a flavored butter that is sure to delight. It's tasty on grilled meats, too!

MAKES 2⅓ CUPS

HANDS-ON 14 MINUTES

TOTAL 14 MINUTES

2   cups (1 pound) salted butter, softened
1   cup sweetened dried cranberries, finely chopped
2   tablespoons Meyer lemon zest plus 1 tablespoon fresh juice (from 1 Meyer lemon)
1   tablespoon honey

Stir together all ingredients until well combined. Divide evenly between 2 (½-pint) jars, or divide evenly between 2 pieces of parchment paper, roll into logs, and tie ends to seal. Chill until ready to use. Serve on warm biscuits or scones.

TIME-SAVER
Compound butter is a cook's flavorful cheat. Freeze slices and store in a ziplock freezer bag to use as a tasty finish to many dishes.

Blood Orange Shrub Mix

A burgeoning craft cocktail movement has ushered in a shrub renaissance with a newfound admiration for "drinking vinegars" or shrubs. Enjoy on its own over ice or mixed into a cocktail as suggested below.

MAKES 3¾ CUPS

HANDS-ON 35 MINUTES

TOTAL 2 DAYS, 45 MINUTES, INCLUDING 2 DAYS CHILLING

1½   cups blood orange juice (from 2 pounds blood oranges)
1   cup granulated sugar
¾   cup apple cider vinegar
1   cup blood orange segments (from 1 pound blood oranges)

Whisk together blood orange juice, sugar, and vinegar until sugar is dissolved, about 2 minutes. Pour into a 1-quart jar or bottle. Add blood orange segments; cover and chill at least 2 days, shaking occasionally.

Serving Instructions: Pour ½ cup shrub mix into a chilled rocks glass filled with ice. Stir in ¼ cup vodka; top with ¼ cup chilled club soda. Garnish with 1 lime peel twist.

Ginger Pickled Pears

Spiced and preserved fruits are a Christmas tradition, but pickling is another wonderful way to preserve winter's harvest. Once pickled, sweet pears become a versatile, savory accent to elevate a roast or cheese plate.

MAKES 2 CUPS

HANDS-ON 35 MINUTES

TOTAL 1 HOUR, 5 MINUTES

2   cups granulated sugar
1½   cups water
1½   cups white vinegar
2   tablespoons whole cloves
1   (2-inch) piece fresh ginger, peeled and thinly sliced
2   (3-inch) cinnamon sticks
3   pounds firm, ripe Bosc pears, peeled and sliced

❶ Combine sugar, water, vinegar, cloves, ginger, and cinnamon sticks in a large saucepan over medium-high. Cook, stirring often, until sugar is dissolved. Reduce heat to medium-low, and simmer 5 minutes. Add pear slices, and cook until just tender, 2 to 3 minutes.

❷ Divide pears and cooking liquid evenly between 2 pint jars, leaving ½ inch of headspace. Cool to room temperature, about 30 minutes. Cover and chill up to 1 week. Serve with barbecue pork or a charcuterie plate.

HAVE A BALL

Leftover jars? All you need to make Mason jar snow globes are jars in assorted sizes (here, 8, 16, and 32 ounces), waterproof superglue, trinkets (we used mini Christmas trees, but anything from ornaments to small toys will work), glycerin (available at crafts stores), and glitter.

INSTRUCTIONS ❶ Use glue to adhere your trinket to the inside of the jar lid. Dry about 24 hours. ❷ Fill jar with enough water to fully submerge the trinket. Add three to five drops of glycerin and desired amount of glitter. ❸ Use glue to adhere lid to the jar's metal screw band. Let dry. ❹ Apply glue to the lid's inner edge, and screw onto jar. Let dry completely before shaking.

LOVE IT? GET IT

We wish to thank the following vendors and artisans whose products were photographed in this book. Source information is accurate at the time of publication. Many items featured in this book are one-of-a-kind or privately owned so not sourced.

Acanthus Studios, acanthusstudios.com
Accent Décor, accentdecor.com
Adventure Marketing, adventuremarketingco.com
Appelman Schauben, appelmanschauben.com
At Home, athome-furnishings.com
Atlanta International Gift & Home Furnishings Market, americasmart.com
Attic Antiques, atticantiquesal.com
BIDK Home, bidkhome.com
Blue Ocean Traders, blueoceantraders.com
Couleur Nature, couleurnature.com
Crate and Barrel, crateandbarrel.com
Creative Co-op, creativecoop.com
Davis Wholesale Florist, daviswholesaleflorist.com
Design Ideas, designideas.net
Designs Combined Inc., shopdci.com
Europe2You, europe2you.com
Gardens of the Blue Ridge, gardensoftheblueridge.com
Hammond's Candies, hammondscandies.com

Hobby Lobby, hobbylobby.com
HomArt, homart.com
Home Depot, homedepot.com
HomeGoods, homegoods.com
L.L. Bean, llbean.com
L'Objet, l-objet.com
Leaf & Petal, leafnpetal.com
Lenox Corporation, lenox.com
Libeco Home Collection, libeco.com
Lowes, lowes.com
Match, match1995.com
Merritt, merrittusa.com
Michaels, michaels.com
MUD Australia, mudaustralia.com
Mud Pie, mud-pie.com
Paper Source, papersource.com
Pine Hill Farms, pinehillfarms.com
Pottery Barn, potterybarn.com
Publix, publix.com
Raz Imports, razimports.com
Roost, roostco.com
Rosse and Associates, Inc., rosseandassociates.com
Sabre, sabre.fr
Sage & Co., teters.com

Saro Lifestyle, sarostore.com
Shiraleah, shiraleah.com
Smith's Variety
Sprouts Market, sprouts.com
Sur La Table, surlatable.com
T.J. Maxx, tjmaxx.tjx.com
Table Matters, table-matters.com
Target, Target.com
Terrain, shopterrain.com
The Fresh Market, thefreshmarket.com
The Silk Purse, Inc., thesilkpurseinc.com
Trader Joes, traderjoes.com
Vagabond Vintage Furnishings, vagabondvintage.com
Vietri, vietri.com
Wayfair, wayfair.com
West Elm, westelm.com
Williams-Sonoma, williams-sonoma.com
Willow Group Ltd., willowgroupltd.com
World Market, worldmarket.com
Z Gallerie, zgallerie.com
Zodax, zodax.com

THANKS TO THESE CONTRIBUTORS

We appreciate the contributions of these local businesses

At Home

Attic Antiques

Bromberg's

Chelsea Antique Mall

Collier's Nursery

Davis Wholesale Florist

Hall's Birmingham Wholesale Florist

Leaf & Petal

Oak Street Garden Shop

Smith's Variety

Table Matters

Tricia's Treasures

Thanks to the following homeowners

The Crane Family

The Gray Family

The Lassiter Family

The Spencer Family

The Tutwiler Family

GENERAL INDEX

METRIC EQUIVALENTS

The recipes that appear in this cookbook use the standard United States method for measuring liquid and dry or solid ingredients (teaspoons, tablespoons, and cups). The information in the following charts is provided to help cooks outside the U.S. successfully use these recipes. All equivalents are approximate.

Metric Equivalents for Different Types of Ingredients

A standard cup measure of a dry or solid ingredient will vary in weight depending on the type of ingredient. A standard cup of liquid is the same volume for any type of liquid. Use the following chart when converting standard cup measures to grams (weight) or milliliters (volume).

Standard Cup	Fine Powder (ex. flour)	Grain (ex. rice)	Granular (ex. sugar)	Liquid Solids (ex. butter)	Liquid (ex. milk)
1	140 g	150 g	190 g	200 g	240 ml
¾	105 g	113 g	143 g	150 g	180 ml
⅔	93 g	100 g	125 g	133 g	160 ml
½	70 g	75 g	95 g	100 g	120 ml
⅓	47 g	50 g	63 g	67 g	80 ml
¼	35 g	38 g	48 g	50 g	60 ml
⅛	18 g	19 g	24 g	25 g	30 ml

Useful Equivalents for Liquid Ingredients by Volume

¼ tsp						=	1 ml		
½ tsp						=	2 ml		
1 tsp						=	5 ml		
3 tsp	=	1 Tbsp			=	½ fl oz	=	15 ml	
		2 Tbsp	=	⅛ cup	=	1 fl oz	=	30 ml	
		4 Tbsp	=	¼ cup	=	2 fl oz	=	60 ml	
		5⅓ Tbsp	=	⅓ cup	=	3 fl oz	=	80 ml	
		8 Tbsp	=	½ cup	=	4 fl oz	=	120 ml	
		10⅔ Tbsp	=	⅔ cup	=	5 fl oz	=	160 ml	
		12 Tbsp	=	¾ cup	=	6 fl oz	=	180 ml	
		16 Tbsp	=	1 cup	=	8 fl oz	=	240 ml	
		1 pt	=	2 cups	=	16 fl oz	=	480 ml	
		1 qt	=	4 cups	=	32 fl oz	=	960 ml	
						33 fl oz	=	1000 ml	= 1 l

Useful Equivalents for Dry Ingredients by Weight

(To convert ounces to grams, multiply the number of ounces by 30.)

1 oz	=	¹⁄₁₆ lb	=	30 g	
4 oz	=	¼ lb	=	120 g	
8 oz	=	½ lb	=	240 g	
12 oz	=	¾ lb	=	360 g	
16 oz	=	1 lb	=	480 g	

Useful Equivalents for Length

(To convert inches to centimeters, multiply the number of inches by 2.5.)

1 in				=	2.5 cm		
6 in	=	½ ft		=	15 cm		
12 in	=	1 ft		=	30 cm		
36 in	=	3 ft	=	1 yd	=	90 cm	
40 in				=	100 cm	=	1 m

Useful Equivalents for Cooking/Oven Temperatures

	Fahrenheit	Celsius	Gas Mark
Freeze water	32° F	0° C	
Room temperature	68° F	20° C	
Boil water	212° F	100° C	
Bake	325° F	160° C	3
	350° F	180° C	4
	375° F	190° C	5
	400° F	200° C	6
	425° F	220° C	7
	450° F	230° C	8
Broil			Grill

RECIPE INDEX

©2017 Time Inc. Books
Published by Oxmoor House, an imprint
of Time Inc. Books
225 Liberty Street, New York, NY 10281

Senior Editor: Katherine Cobbs
Project Editor: Lacie Pinyan
Photo Editor: Paden Reich
Designer: AnnaMaria Jacob
Photographers: Becky Luigart-Stayner, Victor Protasio,
      Hector Manuel Sanchez
Prop Stylists: Kay E. Clarke, Lindsey Lower
Prop Assistant: Phyllis Drennen Lyons
Food Stylists: Emily Caneer, Torie Cox, Katelyn Hardwick,
      Ana Kelly, Catherine Steele
Prop Coordinator: Audrey Davis
Recipe Developers and Testers: Mark Driskill, Tamara Goldis,
      Paige Grandjean, Emily Nabors Hall, Adam Hickman,
      Julia G. Levy, Pam Lolley, Robby Melvin, Callie Nash,
      Kathleen Phillips, Karen Shroeder-Rankin,
      Marianne Williams, Deb Wise, Loren Wood
Assistant Production Director: Sue Chodakiewicz
Assistant Production Manager: Diane Rose Keener
Copy Editors: Donna Baldone, Rebecca Brennan
Proofreader: Adrienne Davis
Indexer: Mary Ann Laurens
Fellows: Helena Joseph, Hailey Middlebrook, Kyle Grace Mills,
      Ivy Odom, Amanda Williams

ISBN-13: 978-0-8487-5226-2
ISSN: 0747-7791

First Edition 2017
Printed in the United States of America
10 9 8 7 6 5 4 3 2 1

We welcome your comments and suggestions
about Time Inc. Books. Please write to us at:
Time Inc. Books
Attention: Book Editors
P.O. Box 62310
Tampa, Florida 33662-2310
(800) 765-6400

Time Inc. Books products may be purchased for business or
promotional use. For information on bulk purchases, please
contact Christi Crowley in the Special Sales Department at
(845) 895-9858.

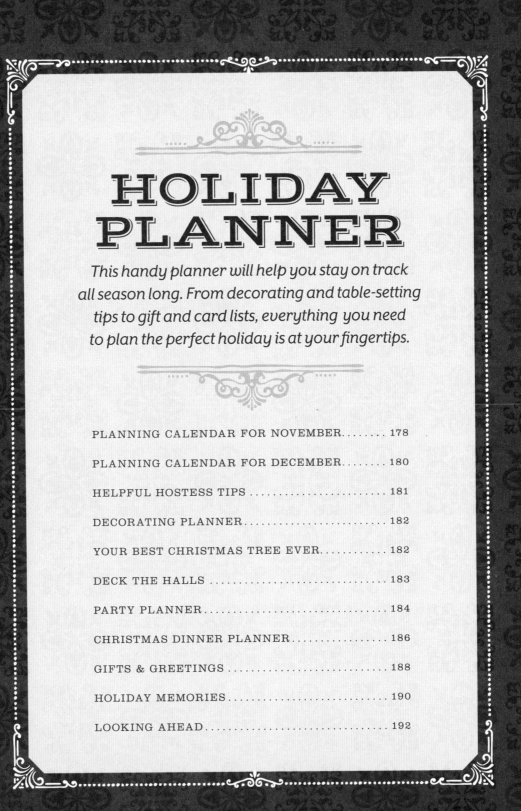

HOLIDAY PLANNER

This handy planner will help you stay on track all season long. From decorating and table-setting tips to gift and card lists, everything you need to plan the perfect holiday is at your fingertips.

NOVEMBER 2017

SUNDAY	MONDAY	TUESDAY	WEDNESDAY
			1
5	6	7	8
12	13	14	15
19	20	21	22
26	27	28	29

THURSDAY	FRIDAY	SATURDAY
2	3	4
9	10	11
16	17	18
Thanksgiving 23	24	25
30		

Holiday-Ready Pantry

Be prepared for seasonal cooking and baking by stocking up on these items.

- ☐ Assorted coffees, teas, hot chocolate, and eggnog
- ☐ Wine, beer, and soft drinks
- ☐ Granulated, brown, and powdered sugars
- ☐ Ground allspice, cinnamon, cloves, ginger, and nutmeg
- ☐ Baking soda and baking powder
- ☐ Seasonal fresh herbs
- ☐ Baking chocolate
- ☐ Semisweet chocolate morsels
- ☐ Assorted nuts
- ☐ Flaked coconut
- ☐ Sweetened condensed milk and evaporated milk
- ☐ Whipping cream
- ☐ Jams, jellies, and preserves
- ☐ Raisins, cranberries, and other fresh or dried fruits
- ☐ Canned pumpkin
- ☐ Frozen/refrigerated bread dough, biscuits, and croissants

Holiday Hotlines

Use these toll-free telephone numbers when you need answers to last-minute food questions.

USDA Meat & Poultry Hotline:
1-888-674-6854

FDA Center for Food Safety:
1-888-723-3366

Butterball Turkey Talk-Line:
1-800-288-8372

Betty Crocker (General Mills):
1-800-446-1898

DECEMBER 2017

SUNDAY	MONDAY	TUESDAY	WEDNESDAY
3	4	5	6
10	11	12	13
17	18	19	20
24 Christmas Eve New Year's Eve 31	Christmas 25	Boxing Day 26	27

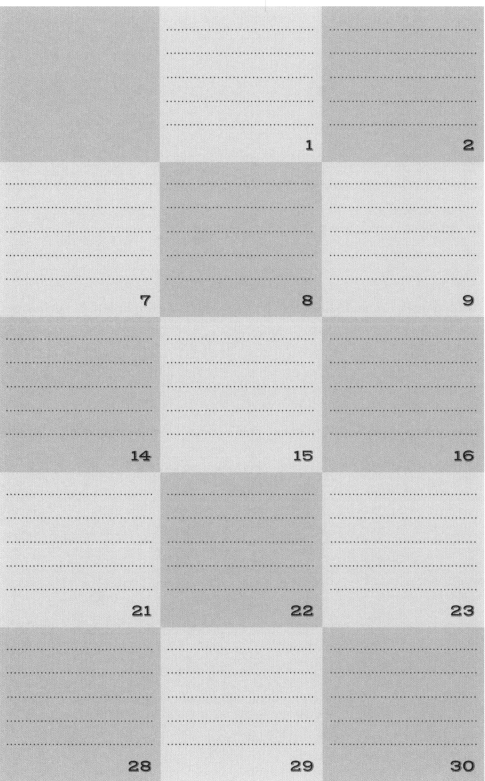

THURSDAY	FRIDAY	SATURDAY
	1	2
7	8	9
14	15	16
21	22	23
28	29	30

Helpful Hostess Tips

Use these shortcuts and tips to make your holiday get-togethers go off without a hitch.

- Always expect the unexpected. Should red wine spill, be prepared with your favorite stain remover. We love Wine Away, available through www.amazon.com.

- In case it rains, keep a few extra umbrellas on hand so your friends don't get soaked running to their cars.

- Think about parking ahead of time. Too many extra cars on the street can be dangerous. Check with your neighbors to see if their driveways may be available.

- If someone asks to help, don't be afraid to take them up on the generous offer.

- Ask friends to arrive with a favorite playlist so you have an eclectic mix to choose from.

- A little prep work goes a long way. Before guests arrive, uncork all the wine bottles, light candles, and put coffee and water in your machine.

- Double check that you have plenty of extra hangers in your coat closet. Or use a spare bedroom to store coats, hats, and purses.

- When hosting a large crowd, consider renting china, silverware, glasses, and more from a local party or event store. You'll be amazed at how low the prices are if you stick to the basics.

DECORATING PLANNER

Here's a list of details and finishing touches you can use to tailor a picture-perfect house this holiday season.

Decorative materials needed

from the yard ....

from around the house ....

from the store ....

other ....

Holiday decorations

for the table ....

for the door ....

for the mantel..

for the staircase ....

other ....

YOUR BEST CHRISTMAS TREE EVER

Several tricks can make your tree sparkle better than ever. Invite these ideas into your tree-trimming traditions, and then sit back and enjoy your gorgeous work of art.

Skip the Usual Metal Stand
This year, use a natural woven basket to hold your Christmas tree. You'll likely still need to support the trunk inside the basket with a stand, but the results are much more beautiful.

More Bang with Bulbs
Lighting the tree doesn't have to be the dreaded task of the season. Go ahead and spring for new lights—there's a much better chance they'll work. Mix large bulbs with smaller ones for extra twinkle, and be sure to use a surge protector with multiple outlets so you don't overload your receptacles with a gaggle of extension cords. Place the lights on your tree at night so it's easier to see where you need to add or take away a strand.

The Real Fun Begins
Start with your largest ornaments first and arrange them all around the tree. If they're extra heavy, secure them to the tree with florist wire. Sometimes oversize baubles tend to slip off branches. Tie inexpensive Christmas balls and metallic jingle bells together with florist wire to create an interesting cluster of color.

Update Your Look
Give your tree a fresh look year after year by editing your ornaments. Maybe you want a color theme, such as all red and gold; then display the rest around the house.

Experiment with Tree Toppers
Bunch fresh holly from the yard and large gold temple bells on top of the tree for a bold use of traditional materials. Fresh flowers are another nice decorating alternative to the traditional star. Or try an oversize bow in red velvet.

Final Touches for a Fantastic Tree
When you're just about done, add some festive ribbon! Use as many colors as you like. Weave ribbon streamers down and around your tree, and secure with florist wire in a few spots.

DECK THE HALLS

Bring joy and merriment into your home with these fun and easy decorating ideas.

Add Color to Your Front Door

Accent a bright white door with the deep colors of an evergreen wreath and garland. Tie on extra-wide red ribbons to complete the Christmas look and add graphic punch. Twinkling lights add a soft glow at night and allow the door and decor to be seen from the street.

Picture-Perfect Garland

Deck your halls with a distinctive—and decidedly charming—family photo garland. Just cut circular shapes from copies of your favorite photos, and glue them to the backs of large wooden curtain rings. Use ribbon to attach the rings to a garland for your stairs or mantel. You could even hang them on your tree. No doubt, Santa will feel most welcome when he sees all those smiling faces.

Fill Cylinders with Ornaments

Use spray paint to add a shimmery touch to pinecones, acorns, or round glass ornaments. Displayed en masse in tall glass vases, they become instant and easy Christmas accents.

Put Out Pretty Pillows

Make a quick switch from everyday to holiday by swapping out your throw pillows. It's an easy and affordable way to redecorate a room and change your look for the Christmas season.

String Lights and Greenery

Disguise unsightly wires from string lights by winding them around a column or post with Christmas greenery or garland.

Create an Arrangement with Fruit and Greenery

Use a glass hurricane or vase to create an arrangement that will last throughout the Christmas season by filling the jar with a layer of limes, red holly berries, and orange citrus. Top it off with stems of greenery.

White and Bright

Here's a Christmas surprise: lilies for your dining room table. Though usually associated with spring, these crisp, snowy flowers with their star-shaped blooms couldn't be more perfect for yuletide celebrations. Available year-round, they add elegance and fragrance to any setting. To create an arrangement, buy one long stem from a local florist. Look for a stem that has one bloom open and several others beginning to unfurl. Clip the flowers from the stem, and place them in a vase. Add water daily, and the flowers should last for a week.

Festive Floor Pillows

Create a comfy spot for kids to open presents on Christmas morning! Whip out your sewing machine and make a set of festive floor cushions, monogrammed with children's names.

PARTY PLANNER

Stay on top of your party plans with this time-saving menu organizer.

GUESTS	WHAT THEY'RE BRINGING	SERVING PIECES NEEDED
....	☐ appetizer ☐ beverage ☐ bread ☐ main dish ☐ side dish ☐ dessert	....
....	☐ appetizer ☐ beverage ☐ bread ☐ main dish ☐ side dish ☐ dessert	....
....	☐ appetizer ☐ beverage ☐ bread ☐ main dish ☐ side dish ☐ dessert	....
....	☐ appetizer ☐ beverage ☐ bread ☐ main dish ☐ side dish ☐ dessert	....
....	☐ appetizer ☐ beverage ☐ bread ☐ main dish ☐ side dish ☐ dessert	....
....	☐ appetizer ☐ beverage ☐ bread ☐ main dish ☐ side dish ☐ dessert	....
....	☐ appetizer ☐ beverage ☐ bread ☐ main dish ☐ side dish ☐ dessert	....
....	☐ appetizer ☐ beverage ☐ bread ☐ main dish ☐ side dish ☐ dessert	....
....	☐ appetizer ☐ beverage ☐ bread ☐ main dish ☐ side dish ☐ dessert	....
....	☐ appetizer ☐ beverage ☐ bread ☐ main dish ☐ side dish ☐ dessert	....
....	☐ appetizer ☐ beverage ☐ bread ☐ main dish ☐ side dish ☐ dessert	....
....	☐ appetizer ☐ beverage ☐ bread ☐ main dish ☐ side dish ☐ dessert	....
....	☐ appetizer ☐ beverage ☐ bread ☐ main dish ☐ side dish ☐ dessert	....
....	☐ appetizer ☐ beverage ☐ bread ☐ main dish ☐ side dish ☐ dessert	....
....	☐ appetizer ☐ beverage ☐ bread ☐ main dish ☐ side dish ☐ dessert	....
....	☐ appetizer ☐ beverage ☐ bread ☐ main dish ☐ side dish ☐ dessert	....
....	☐ appetizer ☐ beverage ☐ bread ☐ main dish ☐ side dish ☐ dessert	....

Party Guest List

....
....
....
....
....
....
....
....
....
....
....
....
....
....
....

Party To-Do List

....
....
....
....
....
....
....
....
....
....
....
....
....

CHRISTMAS DINNER PLANNER

Use this space to create a menu, to-do list, and guest list for your special holiday celebration.

Menu Ideas

....
....
....
....
....
....
....

Dinner To-Do List

....
....
....
....
....
....
....

Christmas Dinner Guest List

....
....
....
....
....
....
....
....

Pantry List

Grocery List

GIFTS & GREETINGS

Keep up with family and friends' sizes, jot down gift ideas, and record purchases in this convenient chart. Also, use it to keep track of addresses for your Christmas card list.

Gift List and Size Charts

NAME/SIZES	GIFT PURCHASED/MADE	SENT

NAME/SIZES **GIFT PURCHASED/MADE** **SENT**

name ....

jeans_____ shirt_____ sweater_____ jacket_____ shoes_____ belt_____

blouse_____ skirt_____ slacks_____ dress_____ suit_____ coat_____

pajamas_____ robe_____ hat_____ gloves_____ ring_____

name ....

jeans_____ shirt_____ sweater_____ jacket_____ shoes_____ belt_____

blouse_____ skirt_____ slacks_____ dress_____ suit_____ coat_____

pajamas_____ robe_____ hat_____ gloves_____ ring_____

name ....

jeans_____ shirt_____ sweater_____ jacket_____ shoes_____ belt_____

blouse_____ skirt_____ slacks_____ dress_____ suit_____ coat_____

pajamas_____ robe_____ hat_____ gloves_____ ring_____

name ....

jeans_____ shirt_____ sweater_____ jacket_____ shoes_____ belt_____

blouse_____ skirt_____ slacks_____ dress_____ suit_____ coat_____

pajamas_____ robe_____ hat_____ gloves_____ ring_____

name ....

jeans_____ shirt_____ sweater_____ jacket_____ shoes_____ belt_____

blouse_____ skirt_____ slacks_____ dress_____ suit_____ coat_____

pajamas_____ robe_____ hat_____ gloves_____ ring_____

name ....

jeans_____ shirt_____ sweater_____ jacket_____ shoes_____ belt_____

blouse_____ skirt_____ slacks_____ dress_____ suit_____ coat_____

pajamas_____ robe_____ hat_____ gloves_____ ring_____

name ....

jeans_____ shirt_____ sweater_____ jacket_____ shoes_____ belt_____

blouse_____ skirt_____ slacks_____ dress_____ suit_____ coat_____

pajamas_____ robe_____ hat_____ gloves_____ ring_____

Christmas Card List

NAME	ADDRESS	SENT

HOLIDAY MEMORIES

Hold on to priceless Christmas memories forever with handwritten recollections of this season's magical moments.

Treasured Traditions

Keep track of your family's favorite holiday customs and pastimes on these lines.

....
....
....
....
....
....
....
....
....
....
....
....
....

Special Holiday Activities

What holiday events do you look forward to year after year? Write them down here.

....
....
....
....
....
....
....
....
....
....
....

Holiday Visits and Visitors

Keep a list of this year's holiday visitors.
Jot down friend and family news as well.

....

....

....

....

....

....

....

....

....

....

....

....

....

....

....

....

....

....

....

....

....

....

....

....

....

This Year's Favorite Recipes

Appetizers and Beverages ....

....

....

....

....

....

Entrées ....

....

....

....

....

Sides and Salads ....

....

....

....

....

Cookies and Candies ....

....

....

....

....

Desserts ....

....

....

....

LOOKING AHEAD

Holiday Wrap-up

Use this checklist to record thank you notes sent for holiday gifts and hospitality.

NAME	GIFT AND/OR EVENT	NOTE SENT
		☐
		☐
		☐
		☐
		☐
		☐
		☐
		☐
		☐
		☐
		☐
		☐
		☐

Notes for Next Year

Write down your ideas for Christmas 2018 on the lines below.